THE HOME DEPOT

BACKYARD PROJECT

PLANS & IDEAS

DREAM IT   BUILD IT

The world's largest and first in home improvement retailer—The Home Depot®—together with HomeStyles, the leader of the home- and project-plan industry, provide the inspiration, the plans, the tools and the materials to fulfill your home-building dreams. Select your deck, backyard project or dream home from our inventory of more than 10,000 plans. When you're ready to build, visit **www.homedepot.com** to locate The Home Depot store nearest you.

For more information on the projects in this book and many others, as well as on thousands of home plans, visit **www.DreamIt-BuildIt.com** or call **1-888-314-1303.**

For additional help with your building or decorating needs, look for these other Home Depot titles:
* *Home Improvement 1-2-3*
* *Outdoor Projects 1-2-3*
* *Decorating 1-2-3*
* *Kitchens & Baths 1-2-3*
* *Wiring 1-2-3*
* *Decks 1-2-3*
* *Landscaping 1-2-3*
More titles are coming soon.

Other titles available in the **Dream-It, Build-It** series:
* *Classic American Home Styles*
* *Deck Plans & Ideas*
* *Shed and Garage Plans & Ideas*

HomeStyles
Founders: Jeff Heegaard and Roger Heegaard
Operations and Project Management: Kyle J. Coolbroth
Sales and Marketing: Jim Plucker

Staff for *Backyard Project Plans & Ideas*
Production Director: Bruce Krause
Managing Editor: Pamela Robertson
Designer: Scott Woodbury
Content: Steve Gramins
Editors: Sara Freund, Josh Kimball
Production: Morgan Brooke, Lynn Colbjornsen

The Home Depot
Marketing Manager: Nathan Ehrlich
Global Product Merchant: Brian Haubenschild
Merchant Assistant: Debbie Cooke
Internet Editor: Anna J. Siefken
Designer: Phil King

St. Remy Media Inc.
President: Pierre Léveillé
Vice President, Finance and Operations: Natalie Watanabe
Managing Editor: Carolyn Jackson
Managing Art Director: Diane Denoncourt
Systems Director: Edward Renaud
Director, Business Development: Christopher Jackson

Staff for *Backyard Project Plans & Ideas*
Senior Editor: Marc Cassini
Senior Editor, Production: Brian Parsons
Art Directors: Francine Lemieux, Robert Paquet
Writer: Robert Labelle
Illustrators: Gilles Beauchemin, Jacques Perrault
Researcher: Lance Blomgren
Photographer: Robert Chartier
Photo Researcher: Linda Bryant
Production Coordinator: Dominique Gagné
Prepress Technician: Jean Angrignon Sirois
Scanner Operator: Martin Francoeur

The following persons also assisted in the preparation of this book:
Danny-Pierre Auger; Ken Balcer, Sandi Construction; Lorraine Doré; Joey Fraser; Gilles Dumais; Patrick Jougla; Solange Laberge; Aldo Parisi; Odette Sévigny; Roxanne Tremblay.

ISBN 1-56547-122-9

BACKYARD PROJECT

PLANS & IDEAS

DREAM IT   BUILD IT

HomeStyles
Saint Paul, Minnesota

St. Remy Media Inc.
Montreal, Quebec

With the right design, even a small city courtyard can be transformed into a tranquil oasis.
(Photo: Jean-Claude Hurni)

FOREWORD

It starts with a dream. A dream of a garden sparkling with color and verdant green. A place where children can grow and play, and for the whole family to gather, have fun or just relax and watch the flowers grow.

Did you know this place was your own backyard? It could be. Today's trends show families are spending more and more time at home. The challenge now is to expand living space into the great outdoors. Backyard structures should have a style and character that enables them to blend in with the family home and become an extension of it. The plans and ideas in this book will help you transform this backyard dream into reality.

Who better to bring you this book than the world's largest home-improvement retailer—The Home Depot—in conjunction with the leader of the home- and project-plan industry, HomeStyles?

Working together, we have developed a truly unique and valuable book that addresses your needs as a do-it-yourselfer. This book includes 24 of the most popular backyard project plans in full detail from HomeStyles, coupled with the suggested materials lists so that you may visit your local Home Depot store and purchase the materials to complete your project. In addition, you'll find lots of ideas that will inspire you to create the perfect outdoor structure.

"The kiss of sun for pardon,
The song of the birds for mirth—
One is nearer God's heart in the garden
Than anywhere else on earth."
Dorothy Gurney 1858-1932, British poet
(Photo: Jean-Claude Hurni)

Contents: THE IDEAS

Contents: THE PLANS

A winding path bordered by flowers and leading under an exquisite arbor entices visitors to discover this backyard's hidden treasures.
(Photo: courtesy Wolmanized® Wood)

DREAM YOUR BACKYARD PROJECT

This gabled gazebo with its Victorian accents is the perfect complement to a backyard water garden. Painted white lattice hides the underpinnings of the foundation as well as the roofing supports, and forms a decorative counterpoint to the structure's traditional white wicker furnishings.
(Photo: Jean-Claude Hurni)

Improving your backyard will not only increase your family's outdoor living space; it can also greatly enhance the beauty of your home. A balance of landscaping and well-constructed, useful structures can really make your backyard bloom. But where can you get the information and inspiration you need to build these dream projects? The plans and ideas in this book will fulfill the information side of the equation, but any project starts with inspiration. Look through the photos on the following pages: They aren't necessarily tied to the plans; rather, they are intended to supply you with vivid examples of creative backyard design. Whether it's a harmonious blend of vines and arbor, a playful house for the kids' corner or a classic gazebo complete with Victorian trim, the following pages—along with the helpful employees at The Home Depot—will help you put a personal stamp on your chosen plan. At the end of the day when the job is done, you may find yourself sitting under the blue summer sky to admire your new backyard— just the right setting to lie back and…dream!

The mail is in! This Swiss chalet-style mailbox, with its attention to detail, greets the mailman—and visitors—with homespun craft and charm.
(Photo: Jean-Claude Hurni)

Who says birds can't dine in style, too? This gazebo-like bird feeder gives your feathered friends a summer spot they'll want to return to.
(Photo: courtesy Wolmanized® Wood)

This vine support combines the principles of a simple lightweight fence with that of an arbor. It also forms the basis for an outdoor lighting station, creating a dramatic nighttime focal point.
(Photo: courtesy Trellis Structures, Beverly, Massachusetts)

Shelter from summer sun or a sudden downpour makes a poolside structure a practical and attractive idea. This gazebo brings a touch of the Victorian to the open expanse of pool and lawn.
(Photo: courtesy Kloter Farms, Inc. / photo by Fred Bird Photography)

OPPOSITE PAGE:
While providing enough rays for sun-thirsty hanging geraniums, this large overhead structure uses simple lath-work to break up the full effects of the sun. In addition, the choice of a reflective white finish gives the setting a light, airy appeal.
(Photo: Jean-Claude Hurni)

The exotic Asian stylings of this backyard ornamental bridge make it the perfect counterpoint to luxurious tropical plantings.
(Photo: courtesy Trellis Structure, Beverly, Massachusetts)

This classic country-style gate and arbor give this row house a touch of individuality and charm. While presenting passersby with an attractive public face, the homeowner reclaims the precious privacy of urban yard space.
(Photo: Jean-Claude Hurni)

Patio islands situated away from the house create cozy back-yard gathering places. This clearing, with its paving bricks laid in concentric circles, reinforces the sense of visual independence. Completing the scene, the round table and four sturdy, outdoor chairs are as inviting as they are practical.
(Photo: Jean-Claude Hurni)

OPPOSITE PAGE:
Perfect for the wild at heart, this backyard setting resembles the overgrown splendor of a field of wildflowers. The rustic arbor/bridge structure, built from debarked, untreated logs, complements the setting.
(Photo: Jean-Claude Hurni)

The robust post-and-beam construction of this combination arbor and overhead gives this backyard its main focal point. Flowering vines are supported by the structure, and surrounding shrubbery serves to soften the structure's massive vertical lines.
(Photo: Jean-Claude Hurni)

OPPOSITE PAGE:
Design means working with what you have. This small, rectangular outdoor space is simply and economically transformed into a Zen garden. The principle of unity is strongly upheld with alternating areas of perpendicularly laid slats. By choosing a white finish and keeping all the elements at ground level, the overall visual space is increased.
(Photo: Jean-Claude Hurni)

ABOVE:
An urban courtyard becomes an inviting rest spot with this Adirondack chair and matching table. The olive green finish, rich yet subdued in tone, both protects the furniture and adds to the setting's cool, lush ambience.
(Photo: Jean-Claude Hurni)

This high privacy fence built from handsome redwood encloses a flourishing urban garden space. It also serves to create an attractive backdrop for potted and hanging plants.
(Photo: Jean-Claude Hurni)

ABOVE: **In any outdoor setting, planters help to give flowering annuals star billing. These finished wooden boxes serve the additional role of creating an attractive divider between two neighboring spaces.**
(Photo: Jean-Claude Hurni)

OPPOSITE PAGE: **In combining the elements of wood and stone, this outdoor design is given an open, natural feel. Outside perimeters are defined with open lattice and foliage, while the overhead structure is built from widely spaced laths, allowing light and breezes to pass freely.**
(Photo: Jean-Claude Hurni)

Children of all ages love to lay claim to their own piece of real estate. But whether you choose a raised fort or an authentic made-to-scale playhouse, think solid. This sturdy pressure-treated structure, with posts sunk into concrete footings, is built to last.
(Photo: Jean-Claude Hurni)

ABOVE: **Benches built into railing structures make a solid counterpoint to this deck perimeter. Bench seats open to reveal handy storage areas, while the corner joint supports an attractive planter.**
(Photo: Jean-Claude Hurni)

OPPOSITE PAGE: **This privacy screen with its "window on the world" makes a complementary addition to this modern home. The massive posts are made to appear lighter with a classic white finish and the surrounding garden softens edges.**
(Photo: Jean-Claude Hurni)

With imagination and whimsy, the effect of this combination trellis, arbor and privacy screen makes a small rooftop space appear bigger. The fascinating structure also supports a two-seater bench.
(Photo: Jean-Claude Hurni)

PLAN YOUR BACKYARD PROJECT

Backyards are like icebergs—compared to the front of the house, they are mostly hidden and unknown. This doesn't mean, however, that your backyard can't be just as beautiful as your home's facade. In fact, a well-designed backyard should be as pleasing to the eye as it is practical.

Of course, it all starts with planning, which begins by assessing assets and needs. Make a list of present backyard activities as well as those you'd like to include. Is a swimming pool in the works? How about outdoor entertaining? And your family's needs aren't written in stone. Think ahead. Children's tastes change as they mature. A sandbox today may be replaced by a tree house tomorrow.

Next, look around the neighborhood. Check out design magazines. Seeing an idea in practice may fuel your own imagination. Now, bring it all together and make a new wish list for your yard. Some of the most popular projects for transforming a backyard are shown below and on page 23.

A lack of foliage may make privacy a high priority. Your first impulse may be to erect a fence around the yard. Depending on its height and the material you choose, a fence can provide both a wall of privacy and an attractive backdrop for a border garden. But there are other options, such as privacy screens, that close off areas while leaving others open. Screens can also be used to divide areas and create outdoor "rooms" (*page 26*).

THE PARTS OF A GAZEBO:
Building Blocks of Design

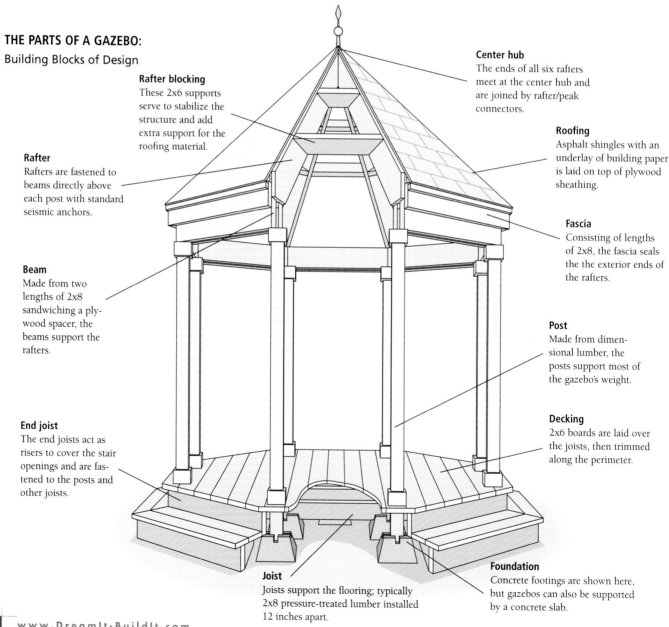

Rafter blocking
These 2x6 supports serve to stabilize the structure and add extra support for the roofing material.

Center hub
The ends of all six rafters meet at the center hub and are joined by rafter/peak connectors.

Roofing
Asphalt shingles with an underlay of building paper is laid on top of plywood sheathing.

Rafter
Rafters are fastened to beams directly above each post with standard seismic anchors.

Fascia
Consisting of lengths of 2x8, the fascia seals the the exterior ends of the rafters.

Beam
Made from two lengths of 2x8 sandwiching a plywood spacer, the beams support the rafters.

Post
Made from dimensional lumber, the posts support most of the gazebo's weight.

End joist
The end joists act as risers to cover the stair openings and are fastened to the posts and other joists.

Decking
2x6 boards are laid over the joists, then trimmed along the perimeter.

Joist
Joists support the flooring; typically 2x8 pressure-treated lumber installed 12 inches apart.

Foundation
Concrete footings are shown here, but gazebos can also be supported by a concrete slab.

A GALLERY OF BACKYARD PROJECTS

In addition to offering privacy, fences and screens also provide a certain amount of shade and can break the wind. For overhead shelter, turn to more complete structures such as arbors and gazebos. One of their main attractions is the ability to bring a sense of indoor comfort outside. Arbors, fences and screens make ideal supports for climbing plants such as vines and ivy, expanding your garden space vertically. Adding greenery to handmade structures will serve to smooth hard edges, blending practical function with the natural elements.

Gazebos, on the other hand, are designed to stand out. Dating as far back as the Renaissance, they served as "viewing pavilions"—shelters for sightseers. Today they symbolize genteel outdoor entertaining, dining or just relaxing and provide a focal point to a garden and a counterpoint to your home itself.

When it comes to the children, assigning one area of your backyard as a "play station" will give youngsters their own special portion of real estate and reserve the rest of the yard for other activities. Sandboxes and playhouses are traditional favorites, and building them with the kids' participation is half the fun.

Other garden accessories, such as planters and furniture, can help supply the finishing touches to harmonize the look of your yard. Planters make ideal borders near decks, patios or along yard perimeters, giving plants or shrubs star billing. A picnic table or a set of chairs or benches also defines a space, creating sections of your yard for lounging or dining, and adding the virtue of portability.

Finally, don't forget the dog! A home-built doghouse will lend a measure of charm to your backyard and complement your other wooden garden structures.

Lounging furniture
Outdoor chairs should be practical as well as comfortable. A tilted backrest makes for a relaxing seat, while wide armrests double as surfaces for cool summer drinks.

Fences and gates
Contrasting two types of fencing material—here, vertical panels and lattice—creates an attractive alternative to a traditional privacy fence; lattice admits light for garden borders.

Picnic table
The portability of this backyard classic makes it the perfect gathering place for a moveable backyard feast.

Arbor
These supports for climbing vines provide attractive ways to create backyard divisions. Vines can be deceptively heavy, however, and arbors need to be built with well-anchored posts.

Playhouse
This child's "room of one's own" should be built to keep the weather out—making it the perfect spot for rainy-day fun.

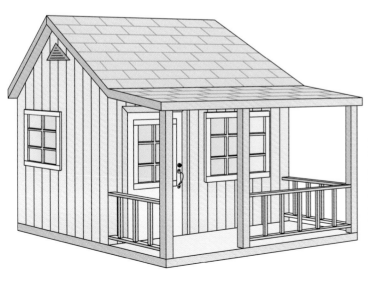

Shape Your Yard

Walking into a well-designed garden is like meeting an interesting and attractive new face, one that imparts intelligence and interest. In nature, these touches of beauty may appear out of nowhere, but landscape design is based on tried-and-true principles that can transform an outdoor space into a creative work of art. Before embarking on your backyard project, try putting pencil to paper to create a backyard plan. Start by looking at and thinking about four basic landscaping design principles: dominance, unity, balance and variety. Throughout the design process, professionals never lose sight of them. The definitions and diagrams below and on page 25 will help clarify these notions for you, but don't end your research here. Try to identify these principles by studying outdoor spaces such as parks or public gardens and see how they've been used. Observe as well the gardens and yards in your neighborhood to see why some layouts work better than others, and how these landscaping DOs and DON'Ts can be applied to your own backyard.

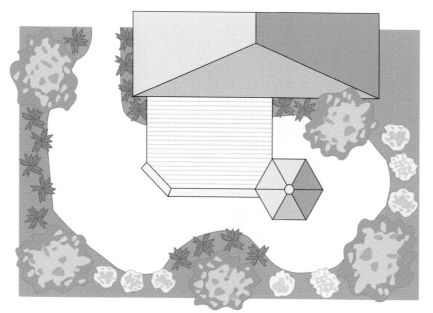

Dominance

Any large element that serves a main focal point is an example of dominance. A dominant element such as an arbor or gazebo helps give a garden its visual center, drawing the observer's eye into the space. An arbor or gazebo can also divide a space or serve as an entryway between two garden sections. Although a garden can have more than one dominant element, no two structures should take a preeminent position in the same visual space. A dominant element should be proportional to the yard area and home. For example, an ornate gazebo may set the perfect visual counterpoint to a large Victorian home, but may outshine a bungalow made up of simple, clean lines.

Balance

The relationship between a backyard's elements and the surrounding space is governed by the principle of balance. Perfect visual balance can take the form of mirrored symmetry, as seen in the formal gardens of the past—for example, identical rows of rose bushes on each side of a walkway. By contemporary standards, this type of balance tends to appear static and contrived. Today the goal of most landscape design is a more subtle and natural form of balance. For example, a gazebo located near one side of a garden need not be matched with an identical structure on the other, but a balancing visual weight can be created with groupings of smaller elements, such as lawn furniture or planters. Color also plays a role. A colorful structure will carry more visual weight than one with a subdued natural wood finish, adding an extra challenge in balancing your design.

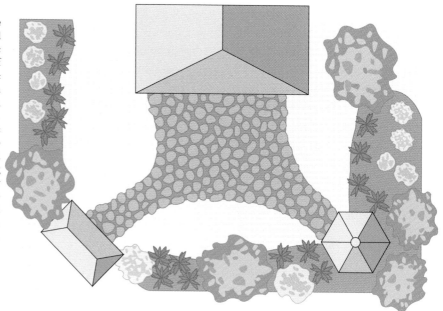

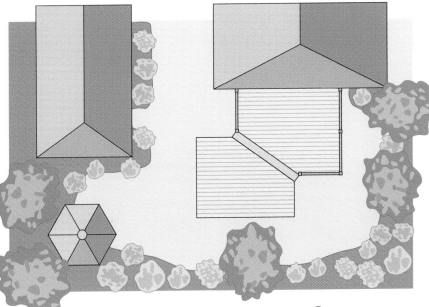

Unity

The principle of unity involves the choice of elements. For example, a unified landscape will rely on a limited number of similar plants, shrubs and trees (rather than balance several types of plants of varying colors). Lawns, patios, perimeter lines and circulation patterns all play roles in uniting garden shapes by creating a strong overall continuity that incorporates even large structures into the unified whole. A harmonious color palette also helps to create a unified garden. For example, using neutral colors such as an eggshell white for all structures from furniture to planters, which are then spaced strategically in a background of green foliage, can do much to unify even the most varied assembly of garden elements.

Variety

Variety is also the essence of a successful backyard design. Even a balanced garden or a unified garden can and should hold a few surprises. Although it may not at first seem the case, the principle of variety is not at odds with these more conservative notions. A backyard with variety, in fact, will help complete the finishing touches after the other principles have been applied. The discovery of a planter or sitting area in a secluded corner or a sudden flash of color amid a setting of green shrubbery can add just the right touch of variety to intrigue the observer and give your garden its most important design element of all: personality.

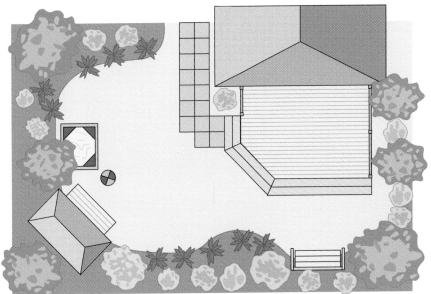

SHAPES AND SIZES

Although the size and shape of your backyard can sometimes seem more of a liability than an asset, with the right design even the oddest shape can be worked to your advantage. For example, the long, narrow space of a townhouse lot can be subdivided into a succession of outdoor "rooms." Each area can then be designed individually so it has a special character. Divisions can also work well for small lots. When the total area is not revealed at first glance, the need to explore will make a small garden seem much larger. Other options include creating new borders within the standard rectangle of a backyard perimeter. "Carving" garden shapes will add visual interest, relaying a feeling of informality and ease. Even garden structures can help reinforce this notion of landscaped shapes. Think of islands and streams harboring garden furniture, a kid's play area or even a quiet retreat, all linked by meandering pathways. The effect: a limited space that seemingly can't be measured in square feet.

(Photo: Jean-Claude Hurni)

Draw Your Plan

Now that you have decided on a list of backyard projects and have had a chance to soak up some landscaping theory, it's time to put pencil to paper and work out your plan. As you do so, remember, drawing a plan doesn't commit you to anything. Have fun with it and let your imagination go. That being said, try to be accurate. The more real information you include on your plan, the easier the job will be later.

This small yard puts existing features to best advantage, blending them with newly added structures to create a unified living space.
(Photo: Jean-Claude Hurni)

The first step is to make a base plan. Working on graph paper, assign each square foot of your property to one square on the paper. Referring to your property deed or lot plan, draw the outside perimeter line of your lot. Next, draw an outline of your house, positioning it within your property lines. Also mark the locations of the lower windows and doors on the house as a reminder of how they may be affected by any new construction outside. Environmental information is equally important. The direction of the sun at different times of the day and what part of your yard is likely to get more daylight will play a significant role in your decision-making process. Indicate shady areas that you're certain of, such as near large trees or areas near the back of the house.

Next, mark the location of overhead power cables as well as any buried utility lines that might be disturbed during your work. Include their depth. If you are unsure about any of this information, contact local utility companies; they should be able to locate any underground utilities on your property. Also note the high and low points of your property to determine drainage and whether some excavation work may be necessary to improve it.

Finally, add existing natural assets—trees, plants and shrubs—that you expect to keep in your new yard and the direction of existing views outside of your property that will also figure in your design.

Your base plan is now ready for your new ideas. To get an accurate idea of how your plan will work in the field, it's best to go back and forth from the drawing board to the site itself. Because the structures you wish to build will facilitate the activities that will take place in your new backyard, locate them on your plan first. Draw balloon sketches—circles marking general surface areas—to locate their possible sites, then get out and take pictures of these areas and keep them with your plan. You can also cordon off the approximate floor-plan size of your new gazebo or playhouse with stakes or chairs just to get a feel of the visual weight of the new space. Garden hose also works well to lay out curved perimeters.

Think of traffic and high-use areas as well. Paving stone or natural fieldstone paths and patios will not only save your lawn in traffic areas, but can form an additional unifying element to your backyard. A patio off the back of the house is a traditional favorite for obvious practical reasons, but a patio nook in a more secluded corner of your yard can create a more intimate getaway area. These elements will also play a role in visually balancing your yard. The right mix of plantings,

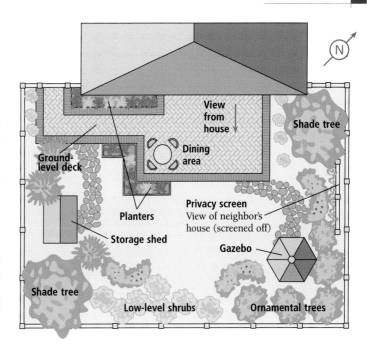

shrubbery and stone make a background within which your new structures can be solidly placed.

Chances are that after a few trials and changes, you'll have to draw up more than one plan before you've found just the right places for your new backyard features. Make sure it is neat and clean enough to be read by someone else; it may serve as a guide for any contractors you hire.

The final plan
Drawn on a grid representing square footage, this plan indicates existing features as well as the placement of proposed new structures.

Legal Ease

Whether you decide to do the job yourself or hire a contractor, some legal aspects need to be taken into consideration to keep your backyard project above board. Building codes and zoning restrictions serve to protect home owners and the community from substandard building practices. Depending on the scope of your project, you'll need to go to your municipal building office with your plans to obtain a permit. Your landscaping plans and the plans in this book should be ade-

quate for most inspectors. The codes governing outdoor structures cover everything from depth of footings and height of railings to sizes and capacities of building materials. Although the plans in this book conform to building codes in most areas and include lists of building materials, you'll need to make sure that the sizes and strengths of the lumber and fasteners you use meet local standards. Standards are fairly uniform throughout the U.S., but there are exceptions.

Zoning restrictions also have an aesthetic side, ensuring that building projects do not disfigure the neighborhood. Setback restrictions determine how close you can build to a neighbor's property line. Lot-coverage limits require that structures do not cover a larger portion of your lot than is allowed and height limits put a cap on how high you can build. Easements are corridors across your property that you can't build on because they provide access to your lot, usually for utility workers. Check your property deed for easements and any other stipulations that govern the design or location of new structures on your property.

Keep your dealings with contractors legal, too. For a major job, it's best to make up a contract that defines the terms. Included in the contract should be a copy of the plans, stipulations on the cost and payment, responsibility for permits and zoning compliance, and terms for suspension or termination of the project. Also add in the contract provisions for lien releases every time you make a payment for labor or materials—otherwise, you could find yourself liable for outstanding amounts owed by the contractor to his or her suppliers.

IN THE ZONE: Restrictions You Should Know About

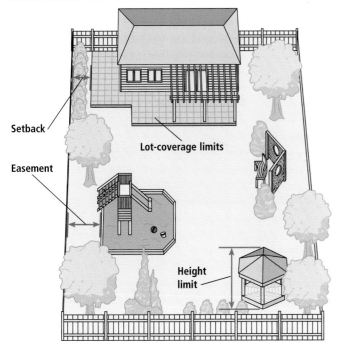

The Road to Building a Project

Backyard projects are naturals for budding weekend warriors. Depending on the difficulty of your choice, a backyard addition can be the perfect project to test novice skills. These two pages are not intended as a step-by-step how-to guide for backyard builders. Rather, they are meant to give you an appreciation of the process and the basic steps involved so you can decide which parts of the construction you feel comfortable enough to execute yourself and which to contract out. Although this book focuses on project design and style, the often overlooked issue of attending to construction details has a huge impact on the final appearance of your project and the overall success of your new backyard.

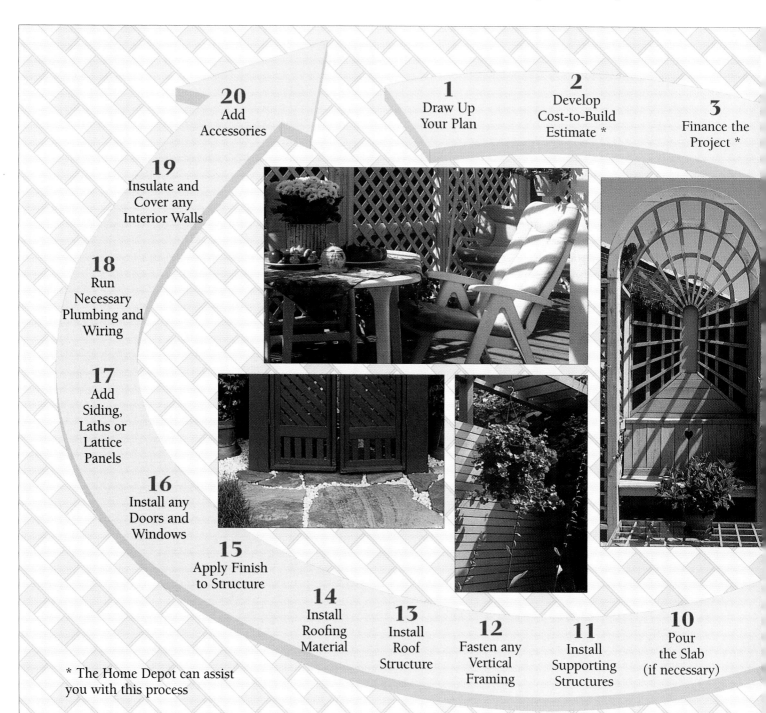

20
Add
Accessories

19
Insulate and
Cover any
Interior Walls

18
Run
Necessary
Plumbing and
Wiring

17
Add
Siding,
Laths or
Lattice
Panels

16
Install any
Doors and
Windows

15
Apply Finish
to Structure

14
Install
Roofing
Material

13
Install
Roof
Structure

12
Fasten any
Vertical
Framing

11
Install
Supporting
Structures

10
Pour
the Slab
(if necessary)

1
Draw Up
Your Plan

2
Develop
Cost-to-Build
Estimate *

3
Finance the
Project *

* The Home Depot can assist
you with this process

4

Take Your Plan
to Building-Permit
Department

5

Hire a
Contractor
(if necessary)

6

Buy
Materials *

7

Lay Out
the Site

8

Dig
Foundation
Holes

9

Lay any
Necessary
Footings

READING THE PLANS

Knowing how to interpret the plans in this book will help you choose the one that's best for you. The plans are all produced to professional standards, clearly indicating the layout, size and position of all the elements making up each project. They are all drawn to scale, which varies from plan to plan. Most of them include the following elements:

• The **RENDERING** is an artist's representation of the finished project.

• The **PLAN VIEW** shows an overhead view of the project. It includes key exterior dimensions and some details, such as the suggested sizes of structural elements.

• In the cases where foundations are necessary, the **PIER LAYOUT** indicates the positions and distances between

the concrete piers that support the structure. Also shown is the process by which these measurements are found—with mason's lines elevated on batterboards. The location of any concrete pad for stairs is also shown. **PER SITE CONDITIONS** indicates the positions and dimensions of any items that depend on the final height of the deck.

• In the **FRAMING PLAN**, the dimensions and types of materials for the understructure are shown. The abbreviation o.c. stands for "on center," meaning that all measurements shown are taken from the center of each structural element to the center of the next one.

• **ELEVATIONS**, also referred to as **SIDE VIEWS**, indicate vertical dimensions as well as types and sizes of materials.

• **DETAILS** reveal the understructure, shown from the side. A below-ground cutaway of the concrete pier is also shown. This view, combined with the other details of the structure, includes all the necessary materials and dimensions.

Although you will very likely find a plan in this book that suits your needs and sense of design for your planned backyard, none of the plans are cast in stone. It's possible to make adjustments to the size or shape of any structure. A rule of thumb for adjusting a plan is to work from the top down, making the necessary changes to the understructure last. Work through all adjustments with a professional designer or builder who will be able to recommend the appropriate structural changes to suit your needs.

Climbing in Style and Safety

Whether you are installing a ceiling electrical box or painting wood siding, you'll need a sturdy ladder to get to the right height. **Werner Co.**, the professional's choice, makes a variety of climbing equipment for your building needs.

Safety is paramount when you are working at heights. If you are climbing an extension ladder, place the ladder at a distance from the wall equal to one-quarter its extended length. If you are using a stepladder, use a ladder that is 2 feet longer than the height you need to stand and place the legs on firm, flat ground.

(Photos: courtesy Werner Co.)

BUY NOW, PAY LATER!

The Home Depot Consumer Credit Account offers a financing solution to your home improvement needs. To make purchases more affordable, take advantage of our special offers and attractive deferred billing programs available only to Home Depot Consumer Account Holders.* Apply for a Consumer Credit Account at any store or online at **homedepot.com** to buy the merchandise that you need today!

*Interest may accrue

MATERIAL WORLD

Along with labor costs, your budget for new backyard structures will mostly be taken up by materials. Wood is the traditional choice for building most of the projects in this book, but a variety of synthetic and composite materials is also available. In making your choice, you will need to balance several, often competing, factors: durability, cost, appearance and design. Concrete for the slabs or piers that support a gazebo or playhouse and the fasteners and connectors that hold them together are also a big part of the equation (*page 35*). Apart from having to withstand the elements year after year, hardware can have a huge impact on design. Fasteners that rust, for example, will stain and decay the surrounding wood. They will also eventually loosen, causing pieces of the structure to give way, posing a safety hazard as well as ruining the look of

WOOD PURCHASING POLICY

The Home Depot is committed to building a better world through sustainable business practices. Responsible wood purchasing is one step toward sustainability and presents a tremendous opportunity to meet our customers' demand for wood products while sustaining the forests for generations to come.

To learn more about The Home Depot's wood purchasing policies, please visit our web site at **www.homedepot.com**.

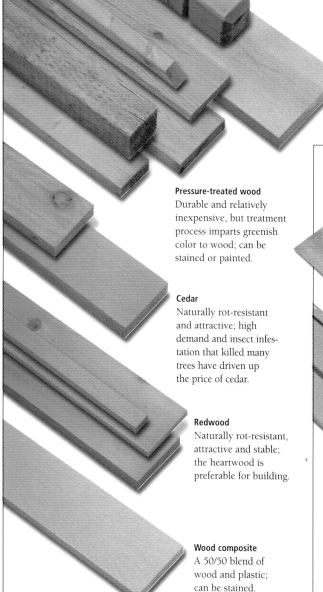

Pressure-treated wood
Durable and relatively inexpensive, but treatment process imparts greenish color to wood; can be stained or painted.

Cedar
Naturally rot-resistant and attractive; high demand and insect infestation that killed many trees have driven up the price of cedar.

Redwood
Naturally rot-resistant, attractive and stable; the heartwood is preferable for building.

Wood composite
A 50/50 blend of wood and plastic; can be stained.

SHED AND PLAYHOUSE SIDING

Cedar
A good choice for creating a rustic look, cedar shingles are relatively expensive and more challenging to install than other types of siding, especially around doors and windows.

Plywood
Sold as T1-11 siding, this option serves double duty as wall sheathing and siding. Because of its large panel size (up to 4 feet wide and 8, 9 or 10 feet long), plywood siding can be installed rapidly.

Vinyl
This type of siding is relatively inexpensive, easy to install and requires virtually no maintenance; however, it is only available in a few colors and is subject to fading over time.

Solid board
Various types of solid board siding are available, including clapboard, tongue-and-groove and shiplap, which imparts a rustic flavor to a shed or playhouse.

This funky bench forgoes the extra strength of pressure-treated wood for a weathered look.
(Photo: Jean-Claude Hurni)

your structure. It's worthwhile getting advice from your local Home Depot associate on the best materials and hardware for your particular project.

BUILDING OUTDOORS WITH WOOD

Pressure-treated wood and naturally decay-resistant woods such as cedar and redwood are the main types of wood to consider for outdoor structures. The chart on the following page compares them. Nothing beats the beautiful natural finish of redwood or cedar; however, pressure-treated wood has become a practical and economical favorite. Although the chemicals that serve to preserve pressure-treated lumber tend to leave a green or brownish tint to the surface, which eventually turns gray, many new finishes have provided backyard builders with some attractive and long-lasting alternatives (*page 32*). The chemicals in treated wood also require you to wear protective clothing when handling or cutting it. Using redwood or cedar for the more visible portions of a structure and pressure-treated wood for the hidden substructure combines economic good sense with the allure of natural beauty.

SYNTHETICS AND COMPOSITES

Synthetic and composite materials are gaining popularity for use in a variety of outdoor projects. Produced mainly with recycled plastics, they are environmentally sound choices. As the plastics contained in these materials do not absorb moisture, they are decay-resistant and maintenance-free.

Many of these materials are usually more expensive than wood, but savings in long-term maintenance will offset initial costs. Both recycled plastic and composite wood materials are currently only available in limited dimensions and colors and they are also heavier than natural wood products. This extra weight has to be taken into account in the building of structural elements that support this material. Your Home Depot associate will be able to advise you on your dimensional lumber needs.

EXTERIOR PLYWOOD

Strong, quick to install and economical, plywood has become a mainstay in building projects. The many grades of plywood range from disposable foundation forms to highly finished sanded plywood, ideal for floors and other visible surfaces. For exterior plywood, choose a suitable "exposure rating." Foundation forms are temporary and the cheapest, untreated sheets will do fine, while pressure-treated sheets are best for roofing or flooring left uncovered by waterproof material. Thicker sheets may be more expensive, but their extra strength requires less structural support than thinner sheets and, depending on your project, may be more economical.

	COLOR	CHARACTERISTICS	COST	USES
Redwood	Heartwood is tawny, reddish; sapwood is lighter-colored	Resistant to rot and attractive; very stable, making warping less likely; can be sanded to produce an extremely smooth surface; heartwood is knot-free; sapwood is not as dense, stable or decay-resistant as heartwood	Relatively expensive	Visible parts of project—railings and stairs; lower grades of sapwood not recommended for decking, but suitable for furniture, trellises or planters
Western red cedar	Reddish brown	Resistant to rot and attractive; brittle and not as strong as redwood	Relatively expensive	Visible parts of project—railings and stairs
Pressure-treated spruce, pine or fir	Preservatives turn wood greenish or brownish; color weathers to a light gray	Widely available in most regions; very durable; typically guaranteed for up to 40 years, provided ends cut during installation are coated with preservative; high resistance to moisture; the most widely used of all wood building materials	A bargain compared to redwood and cedar	Less visible understructure—joists, beams and posts

Rooted to the Ground

A solid future is built on a solid foundation. Look out for the future of your backyard structure by carefully considering this first, crucial step. The illustrations on this page feature common foundation options. The concrete pier is the traditional means of supporting many kinds of outdoor structures. A hole is dug below the frost line—up to 48 inches deep, depending on where you live—a base of crushed stone is shoveled into the hole and a fiber tube form is filled with concrete, giving the pier its cylindrical shape. Concrete that overflows at the bottom of the form creates a wide footing. A metal post anchor (*page 35*) is then embedded in the wet concrete and a post is fastened to the anchor once the concrete sets.

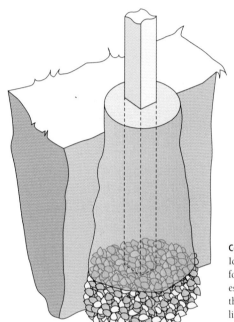

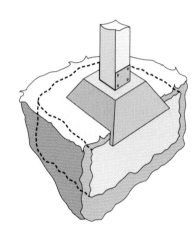

Precast pier block
These units usually come with a post anchor already in place. The block is embedded in a concrete footing atop a wide hole dug below the frost line. This option involves almost as much time and effort as a concrete pier.

Concrete-filled posthole
Ideal for fence or arbor posts, a hole is dug four inches wider than the post and six inches deeper than the frost line. The bottom of the hole should be wider than the top and is lined with a layer of gravel. As with the concrete pier foundation, the concrete should extend a few inches above ground level.

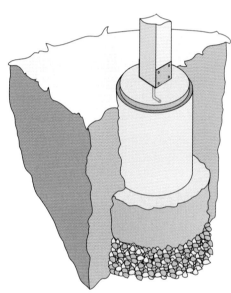

Concrete pier
From the bottom up, this foundation consists of a concrete footing below the frost line on a layer of gravel, a concrete pier poured on site to a few inches above ground level and a post anchor embedded in the pier. This option is labor-intensive.

A Floating Foundation System

Over the life of an outdoor structure the frost heave that occurs in winter can lift its posts from their original positions, causing significant damage to its structural integrity. The standard method for preventing this damage is to anchor the posts to concrete piers dug and poured down to the frost line, with deeper and wider concrete footings at the bottom.

With no holes to dig and no concrete to mix, **DekBrands** floating foundation system offers an easier and less expensive solution to frost-heave damage. As shown in the illustration, the system uses precast piers that sit on top of the ground, moving up and down to accommodate frost movement. The **DekBrands** floating foundation system is strong, durable and safe. Designed in accordance with all national building codes, it far exceeds minimum structural construction requirements when built according to plan.

Precast pier blocks with built-in post anchors also sit in holes dug to the frost line. In this case, however, no tube form is used. Instead, concrete poured into the hole forms a footing and the pier block is set into the wet concrete. As with concrete piers, a post is fastened to the preattached anchor.

Concrete piers that sit directly on the ground offer a work-saving alternative to concrete piers and precast pier blocks. With these "floating foundations," there are no holes to dig or concrete to prepare and pour.

As an alternative to concrete piers, a simple concrete slab will give your structure a solid, even base on which to build and will eliminate the need for supporting posts. If your structure is 12 feet high or less, the slab should be at least 4 inches thick, with a deeper area around the perimeter where the structure's weight is concentrated. Although you can mix your own concrete for your slab, when dealing with an area larger than a cubic yard you're better off having it delivered from a

ready-mix company. Once the concrete has cured, post anchors or sole plates are fastened to the slab with lag bolts. From here on in, the structure can rise with its weight supported by a strong and solid base.

For a more mobile structure, wood skids may be a viable alternative. Used primarily in fairly lightweight construction, any four-sided structure can rest on the two parallel skids. The skids should be made from pressure-treated lumber and set in trenches filled with gravel to ensure good drainage.

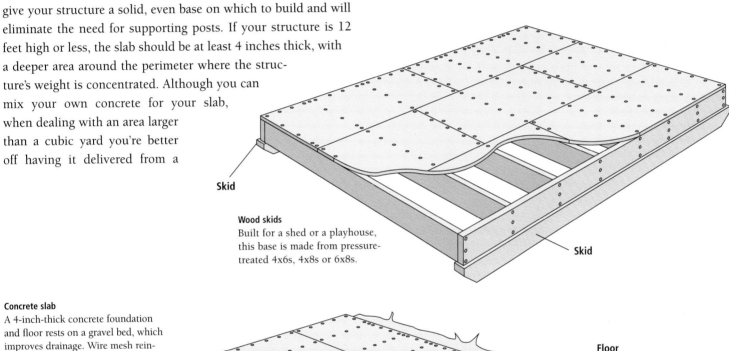

Skid

Wood skids
Built for a shed or a playhouse, this base is made from pressure-treated 4x6s, 4x8s or 6x8s.

Skid

Concrete slab
A 4-inch-thick concrete foundation and floor rests on a gravel bed, which improves drainage. Wire mesh reinforces the concrete and anchor bolts embedded in the concrete are attached to the sill plate to secure the structure to the foundation.

Floor

Joist

Gravel

Wire mesh

Drain tile

Sill plate

Anchor bolt

The Sky's the Limit

Selecting the right roofing material for your garden structure depends both on style and practicality, and can range from the lightweight shade-makers of an arbor to a more substantial roof of asphalt shingles, cedar shakes or slate and tiles.

The examples of roofing materials shown below are suited for roofs that rise more than 3 vertical inches per horizontal foot. Asphalt shingles are an economical choice, offering easy installation and a wide choice of colors. They can also be repaired and replaced easily. For installation, a base of plywood sheathing is usually covered with building paper through which the shingles are nailed. When buying shingles, try to match those of your home and buy extras for repairs.

Cedar shakes make a handsome addition to any wood structure, especially one constructed of cedar or redwood. As with other naturally weather-resistant woods, cedar shakes will last for years when properly installed and finished. For extra weather protection, ask your Home Depot associate about pretreated shakes.

Slate and tile roofing can make an attractive alternative, giving your structure a Mediterranean air. The main concern here is weight. Consult a professional to make sure your structure's framing will provide enough support. Standard roofing slates are sold with prepunched nailing holes and are laid from the eaves upward, with each consecutive row overlapping the last. The terracotta look of clay or concrete tiles is a popular choice, but many other colors are also available.

ROOF MATERIALS

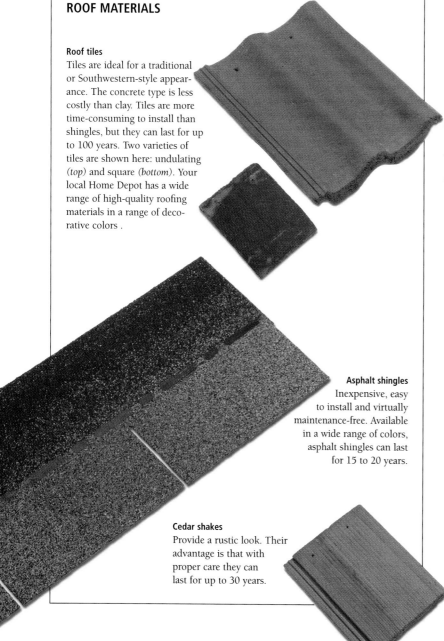

Roof tiles
Tiles are ideal for a traditional or Southwestern-style appearance. The concrete type is less costly than clay. Tiles are more time-consuming to install than shingles, but they can last for up to 100 years. Two varieties of tiles are shown here: undulating (*top*) and square (*bottom*). Your local Home Depot has a wide range of high-quality roofing materials in a range of decorative colors .

Asphalt shingles
Inexpensive, easy to install and virtually maintenance-free. Available in a wide range of colors, asphalt shingles can last for 15 to 20 years.

Cedar shakes
Provide a rustic look. Their advantage is that with proper care they can last for up to 30 years.

Focus on Appearance and Performance

- Ridge shingles
- Ridge vent
- Roof shingles
- Waterproofing underlayment
- Soffit vent

Your home's roof, siding and trim play a major role in the overall appearance and performance of your home. It's the first impression people have of your home and your first line of defense against the elements.

Although your shingles make up the most visible part of your roof, **Owens Corning** makes several other components that are essential to your roof's performance, including waterproofing, ventilation and hip and ridge products. Once you've chosen quality roofing products, you're ready to select color scheme and style. There are many different options available.

Owens Corning also offers a wide selection of high-quality vinyl siding in different profiles, finishes and colors to complement your roof and coordinate with your overall exterior.

Outdoor Hardware

From post anchors holding up the main beams of a gazebo to the joist hangers that support the floor of a child's playhouse, most of the fasteners and connectors shown in the photos at right will never see the light of day once your project is finished. It is these connectors, however, that hold the structural elements together, giving your structure the strength to withstand wind, weather, storms and even seismic activity. But anchors, connectors and hangers not only provide strength at key points in the construction process, they make life easier for backyard builders. For example, a joist cut a little short to fit snugly between the two rim joists of a playhouse floor will not present any problems when it is secured in a joist hanger.

Another important feature of outdoor hardware is corrosion resistance. Rusted metal will stain the wood around it, and corroded fasteners are more likely to loosen and weaken the structure. Galvanized nails and screws, hot-dipped in rust-resistant zinc, are the best way to beat the effects of the outdoors. Their bumpy, silver-gray coating not only seals out the moisture that promotes corrosion, but creates a better bond, reducing the chances of loosening.

When extra strength is vital, especially in the post-and-beam construction of arbors and gazebos, you'll have to turn to bolts and lag screws. Their strength not only comes from increased size, but from the fact that they extend through two joined elements to pull them together from both sides.

OUTDOOR PROJECTS 1-2-3

All of your backyard projects can be completed with the expert advice you'll find in The Home Depot's *Outdoor Projects 1-2-3*. Find out how long your backyard project will take to finish, what to do to avoid common mistakes and how to work smarter with this book's step-by-step and region-specific information that will make your projects last.

CONNECTORS AND FASTENERS

Rafter/crossbeam connectors join roof rafters to beams.

Rafter/peak connectors make up the center hub of the roof peak and connect the converging ends of all the rafters.

Universal or seismic anchors make sturdy connections between perpendicular joints such as between joists and end joists.

Post anchors secure posts to the piers for foundations. The J-bolt is embedded in wet concrete and threaded to the anchor.

Post/beam connectors join beams to the top of posts.

Perimeter board connectors join beams along the perimeter without requiring miter cuts.

Joist hangers secure joists to rim joists for floor structures.

A Well-Connected Backyard Structure

A backyard structure is subjected to a great deal of physical stress. The weather beats on it year after year. The ground under it constantly shifts. And if you live in hurricane country, annual storms put every structural joint to the test. And years from now, the structure is supposed to look as good as the day it was built.

Simpson Strong-Tie makes steel connectors designed to connect, support and strengthen joints in any outdoor structure. From joist hangers that strengthen floors to hurricane ties that anchor the roof to the walls, **Simpson Strong-Tie** connectors make building easier. In addition to adding strength and safety, connectors cut down on the number of nails required for installation and eliminate the need for complicated construction techniques such as toenailing—driving a nail into one piece at a 45-degree angle so the nail tip penetrates an adjoining piece. Although connectors were once optional parts of construction projects, they are now required by building codes in some areas.

Hot-dipped galvanized nails have a thick anti-rust coating that is less likely to flake off than the coating of electroplated nails.

Decking screws have greater holding power than nails and are easier to remove for maintenance and repair.

Hex-head bolts are used to extend all the way through the members being joined, creating a stronger connection than screws.

Sun and Shade

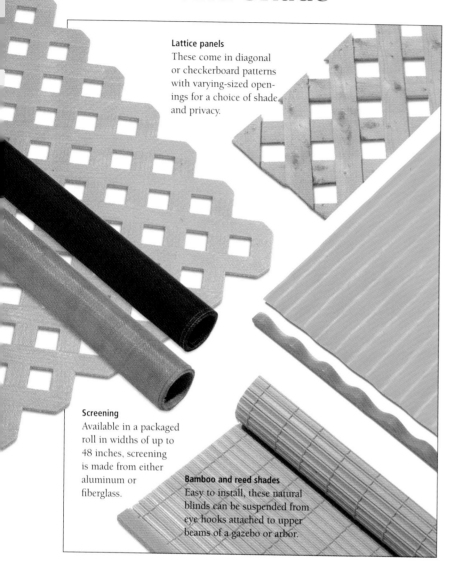

Lattice panels
These come in diagonal or checkerboard patterns with varying-sized openings for a choice of shade and privacy.

Screening
Available in a packaged roll in widths of up to 48 inches, screening is made from either aluminum or fiberglass.

Bamboo and reed shades
Easy to install, these natural blinds can be suspended from eye hooks attached to upper beams of a gazebo or arbor.

Controlling the amount of sun and shade under an arbor or gazebo will increase your backyard structure's livability, enabling you and your family to enjoy its use at any time of the day. Arbors are often built as a support for vines and other climbing plants, but this leafy cover can also form a living roof. Dappled, leaf-filtered sun makes an attractive and enchanting backyard getaway for hot summer afternoons. Without foliage, the open rafters of an arbor may seem to provide the barest minimum in shelter, but depending on the dimension of the lumber you use—ranging from 1x2 laths to 2x8 boards—effects may vary from stripes of sun to an oasis of deep shade. Placing the laths on edge or angling the boards will add an extra element of sun control (*below*).

Other forms of shade protection can be provided with lightweight materials such as lattice panels, shade cloth, bamboo or woven reed, screens and corrugated panels. A versatile favorite, lattice panels deflect the sun's rays while allowing the free passage of air. Shade cloth, made from synthetic fiber, is durable and resistant to moisture. Usually fastened to eye hooks set along the perimeter of an arbor roof, this material can provide shelter for shade-loving plants as well as people. Bamboo or woven reed shades are particularly effective as wall hangings and can lend your outdoor structure a tropical air. They can also be raised or lowered as the need arises, providing privacy as well as shade. The traditional porch screen is another choice, which may be just the thing for keeping insect pests out of the gazebo. Screens also allow air to circulate and soften the sun's glare. A more complete cover from harmful UV rays, corrugated panels make a smart choice for covering children's play areas. Strong and waterproof, they also provide a good place to run for cover out of the rain.

A "Tuff" Alternative for Overheads

Corrugated polycarbonate sheets manufactured by **Suntuf** offer many of wood's advantages and possess several benefits that wood cannot match. Combining light weight with strength, **Suntuf** sheets resist wind and hail and they won't distort in hot weather or become brittle in winter. They are available in a wide variety of transparent, translucent and opaque colors that can suit any design. And while transparent and translucent sheets transmit light with the clarity of glass, they provide protection from harmful ultraviolet rays.

Suntuf sheets are also easy to handle and can be cut and drilled with standard tools.

(Photo: courtesy Elizabeth Benham, Suntuf)

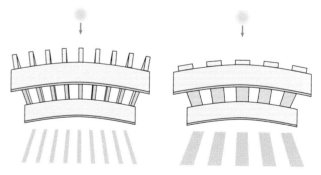

Shade from an overhead
The dimension and orientation of overhead boards determine the amount of shade they provide. When the sun is straight overhead, as shown, boards laid flat will provide more shade; however, boards set on edge will create more shade later or earlier in the day when the sun is angled.

Fancy Add-ons

The possibilities are endless. From gate hinges, handles and other visible hardware to more frivolous flights of fancy such as weather vanes and pink flamingoes, deciding how to decorate your new backyard may only be limited by your imagination. Once you've gotten this far, don't forget your design principles. They apply here, too! Think themes. A sense of unity can be reinforced by choosing accessories in the same family. For example, wrought-iron gate hardware combined with an array of terracotta planters makes the perfect complement to a tile roof you've added to a gazebo. For a more rustic approach, Americana iron weather vanes and gate bells are right at home with cedar shakes and shingles. Balance can be maintained by carefully weighing the effect of your new accessories alongside existing backyard elements. A well-accessorized backyard should never appear cluttered. This does not mean that your accessories should never attract attention. Dominance means focal point, and though your new structure may fill this role, a simple stone pedestal supporting an urn of flowers may also do the trick. Or, why not attract some fine feathered friends? Stone birdbaths can add a classic note akin to that of a formal garden. Art may have a place here. Metal or stone sculpture may not be appropriate for family yards, but if yours is a more tranquil space, why not commission your own outdoor sculpture? And don't forget your sense of fun. This is where the principle of variety comes in. Terracotta masks provide earthy decoration to a wall or privacy fence. A stone sundial discovered among green foliage can give a backyard that special sense of wonder. And perhaps that bed of tall lilies in the far corner is just the place for a solitary pink flamingo!

Wind catcher
Lightweight and colorful, this toucan wind catcher is inserted easily into garden soil.

Wrought-iron holder
This lantern or plant holder stands in a base or can be fastened to a fence or post.

Lantern
With its glass "windows," this Asian-style outdoor candle lantern is virtually windproof.

Fence caps
These finishing touches come in a variety of ornamental styles.

Wrought-iron bell
With this hand-painted accessory, backyard guests can announce their arrival.

Terracotta planter
Embossed with indigenous South American designs, this planter provides a special focal point for large plantings.

Thermometer
This handsome exterior thermometer adds a practical note to backyard decor.

Finish It Off

A good finish should not only increase the beauty of your wooden structure, it should also extend its life. The amount of finishing work you'll need to do depends primarily on the materials you have chosen. Synthetic or composite wood products do not require any finishing at all for maintenance purposes, although they can be stained or painted. Woods such as cedar or redwood are resistant to decay; however, no wood is completely indestructible and the effects of sun and water will show after time. A good finish will seal out moisture, block harmful UV radiation and prevent the breakdown of wood fibers.

Redwood accepts and retains finishes better than most other woods. Semitransparent and weathering stains are the most popular types of finishes for this type of wood since they retain and enhance its natural beauty. Even pressure-treated lumber will last longer if it is finished and its color can be enhanced with most finishes. Solid-stain finishes will help mask the greenish or brownish tinge that is characteristic of pressure-treated lumber and these finishes may be an option for livening up cedar structures that weather a grayish color.

Today's wide variety of exterior finishes also allows back-yard builders to choose from a full spectrum of color and tone. These range from semitransparent stains to solid-color stains, which can either combine with existing wood tone or completely mask original color. In addition to giving your structure a unique design element, pigmented sealants are often more effective for longer periods than clear finishes, providing your new structure with greater protection against the elements, hiding minor imperfections and signs of wear. These finishes generally combine oil-based primers with a latex top coat in one application, a mix that provides the strong adhesion of oil plus the flexibility and excellent color retention of latex. But don't rule out the more traditional exterior paints. You may want to color match structures such as children's playhouses with your home or let your little-home dwellers decide on their own color scheme. Many of today's alkyd or latex paints are ultra durable, stand up to the cold and sun, and are mildew resistant.

No matter what your choice, a sealing finish should be applied to a new structure as soon as possible after construction and many manufacturers recommend treating your lumber before you build. Cut board ends—which may be difficult to get at after assembly—are in greatest need of protection. Follow the manufacturer's instructions for the type of applicator needed and the sealant's drying time.

Although many of today's finishes are long lasting, eventually your structure will need to be refinished. To do so, the surfaces must be prepared. Cleaning and sanding with a belt sander will remove flaking finish, but to complete the job you may require a stripping product. Consult a Home Depot associate about the product best suited to your refinishing needs.

Finishing outdoor structures doesn't necessarily mean retaining the look of wood. Today's designs encourage the use of color, here put to dramatic and thoughtful effect with this Asian-style gateway.
(Photo: Jean-Claude Hurni)

Backyard Upkeep

The amount of care given your backyard will pay off in the long run with fewer costly repairs and a greater life span for your wooden structures. The box below gives some basic pointers on outdoor maintenance. As for seasonal change, the amount of preparation work you'll need to do will depend largely on the climate zone in which you live. For northern zones with heavy snowfalls, take into account that structures with roofs built for summer shade will not be able to withstand the weight of major snow accumulation. Lattice panels can be removed from arbor roofs and stored until the following spring. Even hangings such as those made from reed or bamboo should be removed since changes in temperature can cause them to warp and crack. Fiberglass screens are fairly water-resistant but may tear in strong winter winds. Screens of aluminum are stronger, but are susceptible to corrosion. Both, therefore, should be taken down from gazebo framings and stored away. Garden chairs and benches should also be placed in a sheltered area, while large pieces such as picnic tables can be covered and placed on end, with edges elevated to avoid contact with the ground and spring thaw runoff. For frost protection against your newly planted perennials and arbor vines, check with an associate at your Home Depot gardening center for advice applicable to your planting zone.

The seasonal rituals of care and storage help to retain and renew the beauty of any backyard.
(Photo: Jean-Claude Hurni)

AN OUNCE OF PREVENTION . . .

The work doesn't end when your new backyard structure is built. Daily wear and tear and exposure to the elements will inevitably make their mark. Sunlight breaks down wood fibers. Dirt and moisture encourage rot and mildew growth. But whether it's a gazebo or a doghouse, the good news is that there is a lot you can do to protect and restore outdoor structures. The secret is to keep an eye out for problems and make regular cleaning a part of your routine. Here are some additional tips on how to keep your garden structures in top shape:

- For maximum protection from moisture and the sun's ultraviolet rays, refinish your structure at the intervals suggested by the finish manufacturer, typically every year or two. Before refinishing, prepare the surface thoroughly so the new finish will adhere.
- Reposition furnishings such as benches and planters on a gazebo or arbor regularly to prevent moisture damage on the flooring under them.
- Clean dirt between surface boards with a putty knife or the spray from a garden hose. This will maintain air circulation, preventing moisture and mildew buildup.

- Clean the surfaces of your structures with a solution of water and household detergent applied with a stiff brush. Scrub parallel to the wood grain, then rinse with a hose. If the structure is large, consider renting a power washer. Water at high pressure will help dislodge ground-in surface dirt and clear away debris trapped in gaps. Make sure the washer isn't too powerful—otherwise, you risk peeling up the grain.
- Remove mildew stains with a solution of household liquid bleach and water.
- Because stairs are subjected to heavy traffic, they may need more frequent cleaning and stair treads may need replacement sooner than other components.

- Check surfaces for stains, splinters, splits and popped nails. Set popped nails with a nail set and a hammer or reinforce them with galvanized screws. Remove rust and chemical stains with sodium percarbonate; if that fails, try an oxalic acid-based cleaner.
- To test for rot, insert an awl into any wood surface near the ground. If the wood crumbles instead of splintering, chances are it is rotting and needs to be replaced.
- Warped boards can be flattened by replacing the nails with galvanized screws.

THE BACKYARD GARDENER

From a traditional kitchen garden to a border of dwarf Japanese yew trees, the plants you choose for your new backyard will go a long way in setting the tone, be it formal or friendly. The relationship between your garden and your new backyard structures will also need special consideration. Using the right strategy, planter annuals, shrubs, trees or vines can conceal foundations and generally soften structural edges. When creating a border near a grade-level structure, choose low, spreading shrubs or flowering bushes. Such ground-hugging cover provides textural variety and can also work well when viewed from the raised surface of a gazebo or deck. Plantings can also be used to create a sense of balance in a yard with one large structure. A clump of dwarf birches can be just the right counterpoint to a large decorative arbor. In making your choice, think of the future. It may take several sea-

sons before your plantings reach maturity and achieve their optimum visual effect.

As much as plantings can serve to beautify your backyard structures, the structures can also form the perfect backdrop for your flowers and shrubs. A simple hedge row or a patch of high-growing perennials will benefit from being set against the handsome wooden structure of a fence or privacy screen. The shrubbery species described in the following pages make excellent edgers for lining fences, gazebos or other structures.

The descriptions of these plants—and others highlighted in this section—include the climate zones within which they grow best. These zones, shown in the map below, are determined by their average expected lowest temperatures. Most garden plants have a zone listing. Ask your Home Depot garden center associate for assistance when selecting your plants.

CLIMATE ZONES OF THE U.S.

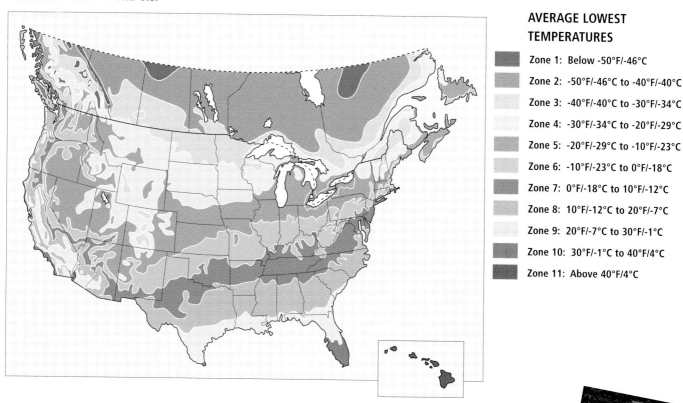

AVERAGE LOWEST TEMPERATURES

Zone 1: Below -50°F/-46°C

Zone 2: -50°F/-46°C to -40°F/-40°C

Zone 3: -40°F/-40°C to -30°F/-34°C

Zone 4: -30°F/-34°C to -20°F/-29°C

Zone 5: -20°F/-29°C to -10°F/-23°C

Zone 6: -10°F/-23°C to 0°F/-18°C

Zone 7: 0°F/-18°C to 10°F/-12°C

Zone 8: 10°F/-12°C to 20°F/-7°C

Zone 9: 20°F/-7°C to 30°F/-1°C

Zone 10: 30°F/-1°C to 40°F/4°C

Zone 11: Above 40°F/4°C

LANDSCAPING 1-2-3

What plants best fit your own backyard? Find your climate zone and everything you need to help you plan, design, select, install and care for your landscape in The Home Depot's *Landscaping 1-2-3*. Specific instructions and detailed plant care guides help you create a healthy and beautiful landscape. Save money and do it yourself.

Color Your Grounds

When it comes to flowering plants, it's all about color. Think of perennials and spring bulbs as the backbone of your beds and summer annuals, with their wide range of continuous blossoms, as decorative accents. But as seductive as a rainbow of color is, large drifts of the same flower species can visually unite different aspects of your garden and make a powerful statement. Backyard unity can also be achieved with plantings of analogous shades—those bordering each other on the spectrum, such as yellow and orange—and can include groupings of different species. Such harmonious settings can be made up of waves of purple crocuses with blue hyacinths or orange anemones with yellow daffodils. Once unity is established, variety can be added. Complementary colors—those of contrasting hues, such as indigo petunias bordered by a ring of fire-orange marigolds—attract the eye and a create a distinc-

tive focal point. In order to orchestrate all this color, timing is everything. Make sure your spring and summer blooms are strategically planted for one to take over from the other.

Planters give your favorite species a special place of importance and provide easy mobility, allowing you to arrange and rearrange your garden to its best advantage. Planters also permit flight indoors when temperatures plunge and fragile perennials need protection. Here's a helpful planter hint: Planter soil dries out more quickly than ground soil—especially when located in direct sunlight. So, choosing soil substitutes that have less weight and greater water retention will help keep your container plants healthy and flourishing throughout the summer. Your Home Depot gardening center associate will be able to advise you on the right container soil for your area and choice of plant species.

EVERGREENS

Rocky Mountain juniper
The blue-green to bright green needles of these conical-shaped trees make them an attractive border shrub.
Zones 4-9

Dwarf false cypress
This compact, yellow-green shrub with thin "thread-leaf" foliage is a favorite for rock gardens.
Zones 6-10

Creeping juniper
Adapting well to city conditions as well as severe temperatures, this shrub is a favorite for its wide-spreading branches and rich, green foliage.
Zones 4-9

Canada yew
Growing 2 to 4 feet in height and about as much in width, this round, dense conifer makes an attractive covering near outdoor structures.
Zones 5-8

Arbor and Trellis Plantings

Imagine a wall—or roof—of sun-dappled greenery. Add to this bouquets of blossoms or hanging bunches of grapes. Welcome to the world of the vine, one of the most decorative and versatile of garden plants. When given the proper support, the shade they provide in a single season of growth can often rival that of a tree decades old. And with the right conditions, they can turn an arbor into a perfumed oasis or a fruitful garden. In order to get the most out of these climbing plants—and make the best choice for your needs—it's important to understand each species' individual traits. Doing so will make the difference between enjoying your vine or battling it for control of your garden. Annual or even biannual prunings are necessary for most vine species, but be careful. As much as vines need to be kept under control, overpruning can ruin the look of a vine, making them elongated and ropy.

Some species, such as the Clematis family—Virginia creeper and honeysuckles—provide less dense shade and need less pruning; and although most cutting is done early in the season, spring-flowering vines such as wisteria, which bloom from buds formed the previous summer, must be pruned only after the flowers fade.

Your vine choice must also be a good match for the structure you wish to provide as support. Some vines with heavy, woody stalks require the sturdy posts of an arbor, while delicate vines need only a trellis or fence. These differing climbing strategies divide vines into three groups: **tendril, twining** and **clinging. Tendrils** are thin, flexible, leafless organs that extend from the vine's body to wrap around a slender support. The laths of a trellis or privacy screen are ideal. Tendril vines include Clematis, grape, melon and pea. To start a tendril

ANNUALS

Begonia
This reliable edging plant does well in both sun or shade. Its white, pink or red flowers bloom throughout the summer.
Zones 3-10

Impatiens
These showy flowers come in shades of pink, lavender, red, purple, yellow and white. They add bright color to shady areas where they do well.
Zones 3-10

PERENNIALS

Purple coneflower
These classic buttonlike flowers with large purple to whitish petals prefer full sun. They like dry soil, so they should be planted in ground that drains well.
Zones 3-9

Lupine
The dense, vertical spikes of these flowers make for great ornamental beds.
Zones 3-10

vine, loop two or three tendrils several times around one of the supports. **Twining** vine species grow in a circular direction—clockwise or counterclockwise—wrapping around a support. They thrive on trellises, but can climb arbor supports as well. Start them by winding branches loosely around the support in the direction in which the species winds—check with your supplier to be sure. **Clinging** vines attach themselves to a support by means of disk-shaped adhesive tips that are actually small aerial rootlets called holdfasts. Best on stone or brick surfaces, they can also attach themselves to dimensional lumber such as that used for arbor posts. The burrowing nature of roots can damage some wood surfaces, so these types of vines should be kept clear of shingles or clapboard.

In spite of these natural climbing tactics, most vines can use a little extra support—especially when they're starting out—and some so-called vines, such as climbing roses, have no natural means of support and must be "trained" by being tied in place. For lightweight vines, plastic-covered wire tied to nails at intervals of 1 to 2 feet or soft twine, rubber bands or reinforced paper ties will be sufficient. For heavier vines, clothesline rope, heavy-rubber ties and pliable insulated wire make good choices. To encourage vines to grow up onto an arbor roof, prune all extraneous branches. Once your vine reaches your arbor's rafters, allow branches to proliferate, loosely weaving them between the upper arbor structure without tying them.

Vines are also good privacy providers. They may not only make a "friendly" natural wall between neighbors, they can also serve to create backyard retreats, green oases that feel miles away from your indoor kitchen.

VINES AND CLIMBING PLANTS

Morning glory
Considered a climbing annual, morning glory can grow as much as 30 feet in one year, with flashy, tubular flowers. It is excellent for covering for open-style fences where privacy is needed. Zones 4-10

Grape vine
These resilient vines can grow throughout the eastern United States. They not only provide attractive cover for arbors and overheads, their ideal nesting cover attracts songbirds. Grapes are usually harvested in August. Zones 3-10

Virginia creeper
The five-fingered leaves of this vine turn brilliant yellow to red in the fall, making it a popular wall and arbor covering. Zones 4-9

Climbing roses
The fragrance and color of climbing roses are a great addition to a garden arbor entranceway. Many climbing roses are hardy enough to survive cold climate zones, but they should be properly prepared for winter. Zones 3-11

Play It Safe

In a child's world of imagination, a backyard playhouse can be transformed into just about anything—a castle, a ship or even a starship! Young play also includes climbing and other acts of daredevilry—fun but sometimes punctuated with inevitable mishaps. Every year thousands of children are injured playing, many badly enough to visit a hospital emergency room, and about one in five of these injuries happens in the victim's own backyard. Falls are the number one cause of these injuries, and preschoolers (1- to 4-year-olds) are especially susceptible. Tumbles during play are unavoidable, but there are several ways you can prevent injuries. Again, it all starts with planning. Placing a play structure too close to another increases the chances of collision. U.S. playground safety standards advise a minimum of 6 feet between play structures.

Choosing from an assortment of cushioning ground covers laid over play areas will also help take some of the sting out of falls and help prevent serious injury. A layer of **hardy grass** will soften the ground surface and retain the overall greenery of your garden. For a more protective cushioned landing place under swings or tree forts, lay a 6- to 12-inch layer of **wood chips** or **sand**. A low wooden retaining wall similar to that of a sandbox will help contain the material. Outdoor moisture and soil will eventually cause wood chips to compress and lose their effect, so replenish and level the area regularly. Moisture also tends to harden and compress sand and since this big sandbox can turn into a play area in itself, it will need refilling from time to time. Other surfacing materials include **pea gravel** or loose **rubber material**. Usually laid approximately 3 inches deep, pea gravel, with its rounded shape, spreads with impact. The trouble with any of these types of material is that they tend to travel and you may soon find wood chips or gravel turning up just about everywhere in your yard—even indoors! A more expensive solution to this problem is rubber gym mats. In addition to providing a soft place to fall, mats make a comfortable rest area and double as an outdoor gym.

Of course, safety also includes making sure that play structures themselves are sound. The playhouses represented in this book conform to building codes for safety; however, the wear and tear of play means structures need to be built tough to last. Extra attention should be paid to foundations, making sure piers are sturdy and well anchored. When it comes to hardware and fasteners, your Home Depot associate can help you make some smart choices. Carriage bolts, with their rounded heads, prevent snags on clothing, while employing hidden fastener systems removes the hazards of nail and screw heads. Using the best and latest framing connectors increases your structure's strength and sturdiness. Universal or seismic anchors, made to handle the rigors of the elements, are good choices for keeping up with youthful energy.

The right choice of ground cover can make the difference between soft and hard landings during summertime play.
(Photo: Jean-Claude Hurni)

PRESSURE-TREATED LUMBER
Safety Alert!

Always wear eye protection, a dust mask and long clothes when cutting and handling pressure-treated lumber. Be sure you are working safely by checking out the important handling tips at **www.epa.gov/opp00001/citizens/1file.htm.**

BACKYARD SAFETY TIPS:

- Install a gate at your playhouse entrance to prevent unsupervised play.
- Remove any drawstrings from children's clothing before they venture onto the playhouse.
- Keep clotheslines and other in-the-air obstructions well out of reach.
- Potting sheds and toolsheds should be locked; toxic materials such as pesticides or paint thinner should be kept well out of the way in a childproof storage area.
- Make upkeep and maintenance of your children's play structures a part of your seasonal routine.

Creature Comforts

Once an oft-seen part of the family home, the good old dog-house had all but disappeared from the American scene. Lately, though, the idea of giving Fido his own patch of real estate seems to be coming back into vogue. Many dog owners contend that dogs "started" in their own shelters learn to prefer them to other parts of the home and some breeds, such as pointers, enjoy a keener sense of smell when permitted to spend more time out of doors. The doghouse in our plans (*see page 71*) is a simple, but elegant frame construction covered with tongue-in-groove siding. The fun thing about building your own doghouse, however, is adding your own special touches, making your best friend feel his or her home is as personalized as your own. Dog abodes of a previous era can lend some inspiration. Stately Victorian homes were matched with Victorian pooch palaces, complete with gingerbread trim. Other popular styles were mock Tudor or even solid brick with cedar-shake roofs and (non-working) chimneys. You don't have to go that far. A stained finish or handsome coat of paint to harmonize your pet's home with your own, plus a monikered shingle attesting to ownership, may be all you need in terms of decor.

Think also, of course, of shelter. Your dog's new home should be warm and dry. As with your own home, keeping weather out means paying special attention to the roof. Lay a strip of aluminum flashing along the roof's apex. Standard roofing shingles make an excellent covering, as do natural or synthetic cedar shakes. Joints between the roof and walls should be sealed with exterior caulk. Using hot-dipped galvanized or stainless-steel fasteners keeps rust from staining the surface and rotting the wood construction. Situating the house out of direct sun and locating a vent at the back to provide air circulation will keep it cool in summer. Interior amenities such as a warm rug make an appreciated layer of insulation and give your dog the "scents" of home.

Creating a backyard area for your dog doesn't end with building a doghouse. As with your child's play area, Fido needs his own space. An enclosed dog run or kennel can provide exercise space without tearing up the rest of the yard. A minimum of 6 feet in width is generally recommended, with the length of the kennel equal to the depth of the yard. Enclosing the area with slender wrought-iron balusters strung between wooden posts can give a rustic and pleasing appearance to the area, remaining visually open enough to allow your dog to still feel connected to other activities in the yard.

Matching your best friend's abode with his size will make him feel more secure and help to keep his home warm in cool weather.
(Photo: courtesy Wolmanized® Wood)

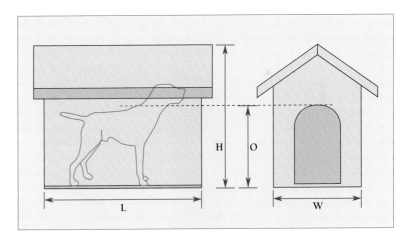

Who let the dogs out?
A rule of thumb in determining doghouse dimensions is to make the length of the structure (L) one-and-a-half times that of your full-grown dog (excluding the tail), while the width (W) should be two-thirds of the dog's length. The structure's height (H) ought to be one-fifth greater than the distance from the top of the dog's head to the ground. The opening (O) should just clear shoulder height.

Light Up the Night

A warm ambience turns this attractive arbor into a welcome gathering spot long after sunset.
(Photo: Jean-Claude Hurni)

Enjoying the use of your new backyard shouldn't end at sundown. Adding light to the outdoors can not only transform your garden into a fully functioning nighttime space, it can add a special touch of drama and magic. Outdoor lighting can be divided into three categories according to purpose: safety and security, recreational space, and mood and decoration.

To decide how much lighting your backyard needs, try this experiment. Venture out after dark with a flashlight. Shine the light in different directions and spots in the yard. Angle the light up and down for different effects. Remember the plan you made before you started your backyard renovations? Still got it? Good. Lay tracing paper over it—this will be your outdoor lighting planner. Based on your tests outside, mark your new plan with some of the spots you'd like to illuminate. Once these areas are highlighted, you can think about the types of light

available and which ones best suit your needs. Overhead floodlights are practical for large areas and are ideal for security purposes. One floodlight placed centrally above the back entrance or a light placed at each corner of the house will provide ample overall illumination. Floodlights equipped with motion detectors turn on when someone passes through the yard, welcoming guests or discouraging intruders. They can also be focused on activity areas—such as over the grill—where good lighting is essential.

For more sophisticated mood lighting, most backyard designers turn to low-voltage fixtures. Available in 12-volt system kits that include a transformer, low-voltage lighting in most cases does not require a permit for installation. Here's a simple test for planning your low-voltage system: Light a few candles and place them in spots you think need the most light. Move them around. Add more if necessary. This will give you an idea of how much light these fixtures supply and where they'll work best.

The types of lighting shown on these pages are just some examples of the styles available. Post lights, which are permanent fixtures with buried wiring, are ideal for paths and driveways. In addition to ambience and safety, low-voltage lighting systems can also erase shadows in dark corners, providing your backyard with additional security. They can also provide sufficient lighting for recreation areas that do not require bright illumination. When lighting an area such as a gazebo or arbor, the

LET THERE BE LIGHT

The 120-volt outdoor floodlight shown at the far right adds a level of safety and security to the backyard area. Motion detectors or photocells automatically turn the light on at dusk or when movement is detected. Low-voltage lights frequently come pole-mounted and can be simply stuck in the ground to light paths from your backyard structure to the house. Other types of low-voltage fixtures can be mounted onto structures with brackets, accenting edges or railings. Rope lights are a great decorative option for this purpose. Sold in 12- to 16-foot lengths, they can be installed along any horizontal or vertical surface.

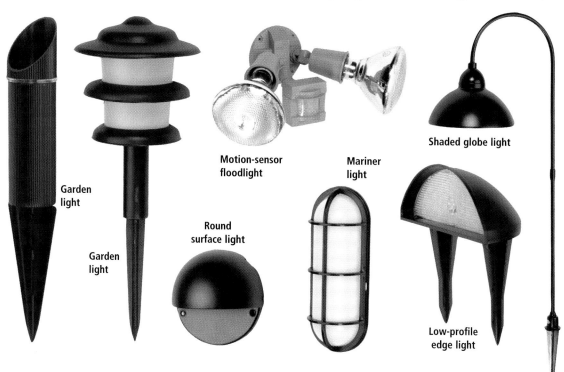

Garden light

Garden light

Motion-sensor floodlight

Round surface light

Mariner light

Shaded globe light

Low-profile edge light

THE SIMPLICITY OF LOW-VOLTAGE OUTDOOR LIGHTING SYSTEMS

The "low-voltage" in a low-voltage lighting system is provided by a transformer that steps 120-volt household current down to 12 volts. Many low-voltage lighting kits are simply plugged into a standard outlet. Because of moisture, code requires all outdoor outlets to be protected by a ground-fault circuit interrupter (GFCI). GFCIs shut off power to a circuit virtually the instant a ground leak is detected, preventing you from receiving a potentially fatal shock. As for connecting the lights, low-voltage systems are simple to install. They generally have a two-wire cable that connects to the fixtures without stripping or splicing. The transformer should be installed in a sheltered area at least 1 foot above ground.

Freestanding and portable, a "mushroom" heater can be put where it is most needed. When not in use, it should be stored in a dry place.
(Photo: courtesy RMC International, Denver, Colorado)

structure itself can be used to support and enhance the effects of the lighting. Fixtures attached to posts and railings define the structure's shape, while illuminated gazebo rafters make for a striking play of light and shadow. And you don't need a special occasion to add a festive air. Traditional Chinese lanterns or more unusual lighting designs such as rope lights can provide just the right elements to give your nighttime garden that special touch of magic.

WIRING 1-2-3

Learn how to install new fixtures, run cable, add circuits or rewire and detach old wires in The Home Depot's *Wiring 1-2-3*. In addition, find out how to select the best materials for your shed, garage or other project and how to avoid common mistakes.

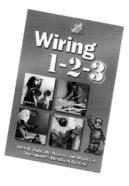

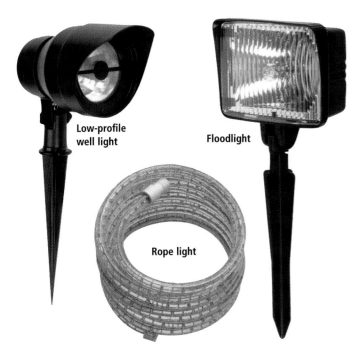

Low-profile well light

Floodlight

Rope light

Turning Up the Heat

Besides light, the other necessity to keeping your outdoor space comfortable is heat. Cool summer evenings and brisk autumn days may prove a little too chilly for sitting outside. Bringing a little heat into the picture may be just the thing to allow you to extend the use of your backyard. Fire pits have been used since prehistoric times and kept early *homo sapiens* warm on the primordial plains. They may also do the trick in your backyard. Permanent fire pit settings in stone or brick can make an attractive focal point; however, metal or pottery braziers permit portability, a bonus for small yards where you may not want to use precious space on a permanent fire pit. In either case, safety must come first. Positioning the fire well away from any structure that could be ignited by flying sparks is essential. Check your local regulations concerning outdoor fires; in many localities, a permit is required.

Another heating option is outdoor gas heaters. One of the most powerful of these is the freestanding or "mushroom" heater that can effectively provide a comfort zone of 12 to 15 feet in diameter. Propane is stored in the wide base of the structure, while the reflective mushroom "hat" radiates heat downward. Another option, mounted directional heaters, are especially useful on a semi-enclosed structure such as an arbor, gazebo or tall fence. The structure not only supports the heater, it can also help prevent the generated heat from dissipating in prevailing winds.

OUR MOST POPULAR BACKYARD PROJECT PLANS

In the pages that follow we present our most popular backyard project plans. Our selection includes a variety of options and styles so you can adapt your project to your own backyard, your needs and even the style of your home. From a classic picnic table to a Victorian-style gazebo, there are projects here to suit every backyard and every budget. Each plan, be it for a playhouse, an arbor or outdoor furniture, is followed by a complete construction plan and material list. Depending on the complexity of the structure, the following drawings are included:

- Plan Rendering
- Plan View
- Pier Layout
- Framing Plan
- Elevations
- Details

Once you've selected the plan you'd like to build, take the material list to your local Home Depot store to purchase everything you'll need to begin construction.

> "He who plans and follows out that plan, carries a thread that will guide him through the maze of the most busy life. But where no plan is laid, chaos will soon reign."
> Victor Hugo
> (Photo: courtesy Kloter Farms, Inc. / photo by Fred Bird Photography)

To get more information on these plans or to see our other project plans, visit us at **www.DreamIt-BuildIt.com**, where you'll find these additional building aides:

- A comprehensive list of recommended materials
- A tools list
- "Build-It Guide" with illustrations
- Tips on how to build your project smarter and safer
- A glossary of project-related building terms

To see the quality of our complete project plans, download our FREE doghouse plan. Our site also offers the largest on-line inventory of home plans. **Call 1-888-314-1303 for more information.**

DISCLAIMER

Building Codes: Variations in building codes, specific local development covenants or site conditions may require modification to the design of the project plans and other information contained in this publication. You are ultimately responsible for complying with all applicable permit, building codes and other regulatory requirements. Be sure to review the plans with your local building inspector and acquire all appropriate building permits before starting your project. The project plans have been designed in accordance with the Uniform Building Code (UBC 1997).

Accuracy: There always exists a possibility for errors or omissions in the project plans and other information contained in this publication. Therefore, you and/or your building contractor(s) shall assume the responsibility of verifying all conditions and dimensions contained within a project plan prior to the start of construction. Please report any discrepancies to HomeStyles, Inc. at 1-888-314-1303 for verification and/or correction before proceeding with construction. You and/or your building contractor(s) shall assume responsibility for errors that are not reported. HomeStyles'

warranty for errors and omissions is limited to, and may not exceed, the amount of fees collected for the design services related to the purchase of these plans. The Home Depot, Inc. and its directors, officers, employees, affiliates and subsidiaries specifically disclaim all warranties and conditions of any kind.

Liability: Neither The Home Depot, Inc. and its directors, officers, employees, affiliates and subsidiaries nor HomeStyles shall have any liability or responsibility for your action or inaction in connection with any project plan or any other information contained in this publication or for any damage or liability that arises during the construction and/or use of any project or project plan. Always read and observe all of the safety precautions provided by any tool or equipment manufacturer and follow all accepted safety procedures.

Materials Lists: Materials Lists are based upon the drawings contained in this plan set. Actual quantities may vary based upon actual site conditions.

THE ROCHESTER

HPM-1502

This simple playhouse plan promises hours of fun and imaginative play for the kids. A shingled roof protects the interior, while three windows let in natural light. At 48 sq. ft., there's enough room for the oversized kitchen toys that used to take up space inside your home. The flower box is a welcoming addition. (Note: Play furniture is not included in the plan.)

Dimensions for this playhouse are 8' X 6'.

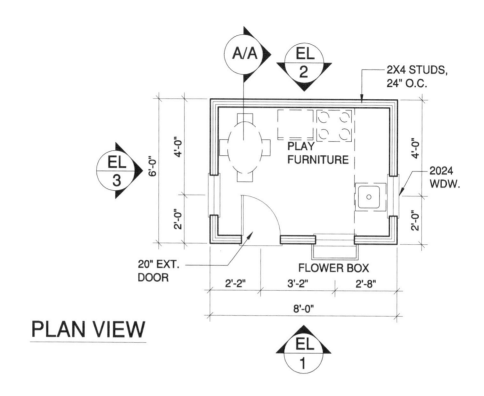

PLAN VIEW

Labels within Plan View:
- A/A
- EL 2
- EL 3
- EL 1
- 2X4 STUDS, 24" O.C.
- 2024 WDW.
- PLAY FURNITURE
- FLOWER BOX
- 20" EXT. DOOR
- 4'-0"
- 2'-0"
- 6'-0"
- 2'-2" 3'-2" 2'-8"
- 8'-0"

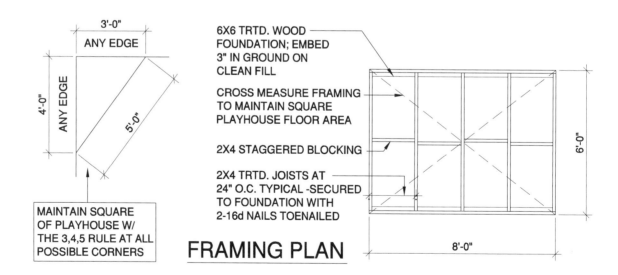

FRAMING PLAN

Labels within Framing Plan:
- 3'-0"
- ANY EDGE
- 4'-0"
- ANY EDGE
- 5'-0"
- MAINTAIN SQUARE OF PLAYHOUSE W/ THE 3,4,5 RULE AT ALL POSSIBLE CORNERS
- 6X6 TRTD. WOOD FOUNDATION; EMBED 3" IN GROUND ON CLEAN FILL
- CROSS MEASURE FRAMING TO MAINTAIN SQUARE PLAYHOUSE FLOOR AREA
- 2X4 STAGGERED BLOCKING
- 2X4 TRTD. JOISTS AT 24" O.C. TYPICAL -SECURED TO FOUNDATION WITH 2-16d NAILS TOENAILED
- 6'-0"
- 8'-0"

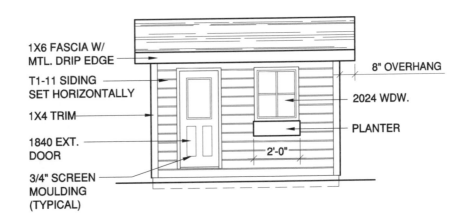

1X6 FASCIA W/
MTL. DRIP EDGE

T1-11 SIDING
SET HORIZONTALLY

1X4 TRIM

1840 EXT.
DOOR

3/4" SCREEN
MOULDING
(TYPICAL)

8" OVERHANG

2024 WDW.

PLANTER

2'-0"

EL 1 FRONT ELEVATION

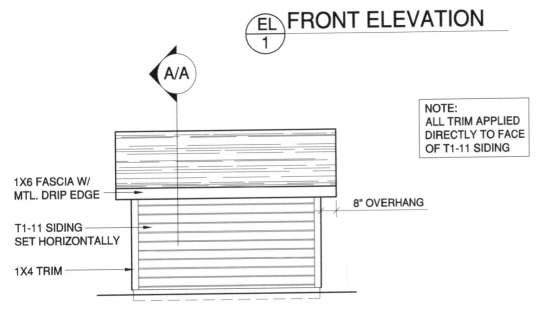

A/A

1X6 FASCIA W/
MTL. DRIP EDGE

T1-11 SIDING
SET HORIZONTALLY

1X4 TRIM

8" OVERHANG

NOTE:
ALL TRIM APPLIED
DIRECTLY TO FACE
OF T1-11 SIDING

EL 2 REAR ELEVATION

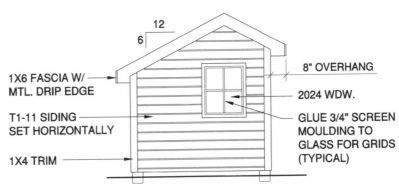

6 12

1X6 FASCIA W/
MTL. DRIP EDGE

T1-11 SIDING
SET HORIZONTALLY

1X4 TRIM

8" OVERHANG

2024 WDW.

GLUE 3/4" SCREEN
MOULDING TO
GLASS FOR GRIDS
(TYPICAL)

EL 3 LEFT ELEVATION

RIGHT ELEVATION
REVERSE OF LEFT

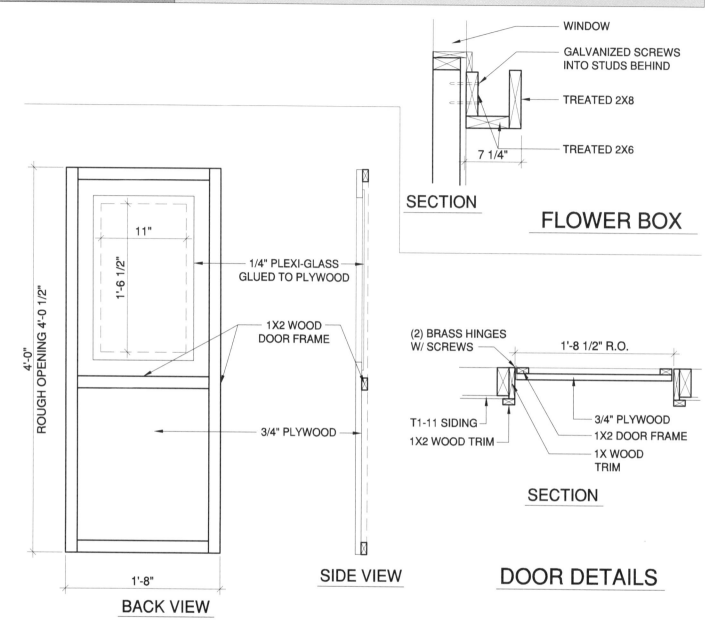

WINDOW

GALVANIZED SCREWS
INTO STUDS BEHIND

TREATED 2X8

TREATED 2X6

7 1/4"

SECTION

FLOWER BOX

1/4" PLEXI-GLASS
GLUED TO PLYWOOD

11"

1'-6 1/2"

ROUGH OPENING 4'-0 1/2"

4'-0"

1X2 WOOD
DOOR FRAME

3/4" PLYWOOD

1'-8"

BACK VIEW

SIDE VIEW

(2) BRASS HINGES
W/ SCREWS

1'-8 1/2" R.O.

T1-11 SIDING

1X2 WOOD TRIM

3/4" PLYWOOD

1X2 DOOR FRAME

1X WOOD
TRIM

SECTION

DOOR DETAILS

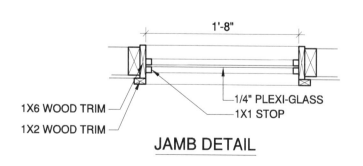

1'-8"

1X6 WOOD TRIM

1X2 WOOD TRIM

1/4" PLEXI-GLASS

1X1 STOP

JAMB DETAIL

WINDOW DETAILS

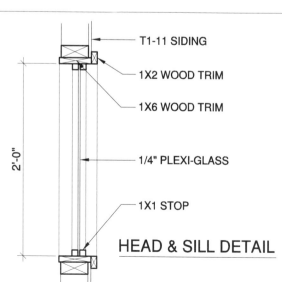

T1-11 SIDING

1X2 WOOD TRIM

1X6 WOOD TRIM

1/4" PLEXI-GLASS

1X1 STOP

2'-0"

HEAD & SILL DETAIL

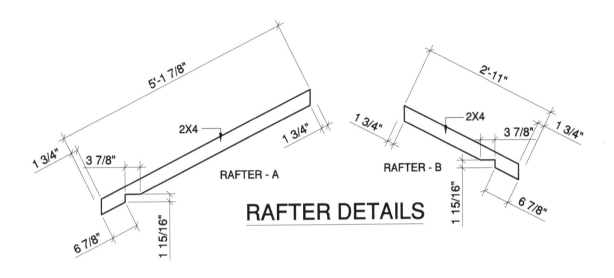

5'-1 7/8"

1 3/4"

3 7/8"

2X4

1 3/4"

RAFTER - A

6 7/8"

1 15/16"

2'-11"

1 3/4"

2X4

3 7/8"

1 3/4"

RAFTER - B

1 15/16"

6 7/8"

RAFTER DETAILS

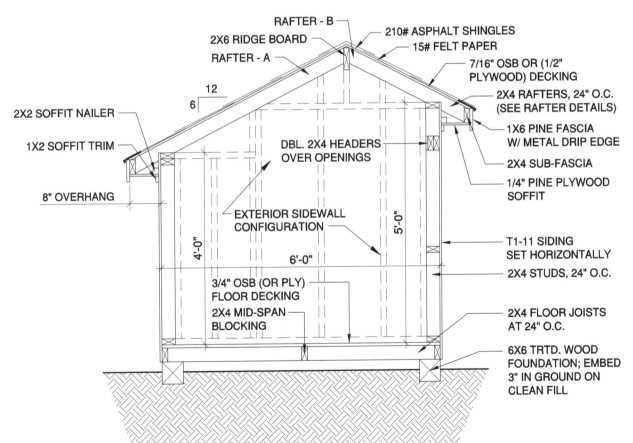

RAFTER - B

2X6 RIDGE BOARD

RAFTER - A

210# ASPHALT SHINGLES

15# FELT PAPER

7/16" OSB OR (1/2"
PLYWOOD) DECKING

2X4 RAFTERS, 24" O.C.
(SEE RAFTER DETAILS)

2X2 SOFFIT NAILER

1X2 SOFFIT TRIM

8" OVERHANG

12

6

DBL. 2X4 HEADERS
OVER OPENINGS

1X6 PINE FASCIA
W/ METAL DRIP EDGE

2X4 SUB-FASCIA

1/4" PINE PLYWOOD
SOFFIT

EXTERIOR SIDEWALL
CONFIGURATION

4'-0"

5'-0"

6'-0"

3/4" OSB (OR PLY)
FLOOR DECKING

2X4 MID-SPAN
BLOCKING

T1-11 SIDING
SET HORIZONTALLY

2X4 STUDS, 24" O.C.

2X4 FLOOR JOISTS
AT 24" O.C.

6X6 TRTD. WOOD
FOUNDATION; EMBED
3" IN GROUND ON
CLEAN FILL

(A-A) **CROSS SECTION**

FOUNDATION

Item	Location	Qty	UM
6x6 - 8' Treated	Foundation	2	EA

FLOOR

Item	Location	Qty	UM
2x4 - 8' Treated	Joist/Blocking	4	EA
2x4 - 12' Treated	Joist	2	EA
3/4" OSB (Ply.)	Floor Decking	2	EA
5# 16d Galv. Nails	General Framing	1	EA
5# 8d Ctd. Box Nails	General Framing	1	EA
1# 2-1/2" Ctd. Ext. Screws	Floor Decking	1	EA

WALL FRAMING

Item	Location	Qty	UM
2x4 - 8' Std. & Btr.	Top/Bottom Plate	4	EA
2x4 - 12' Std. & Btr.	Top/Bottom Plate	2	EA
2x4 - 8' Std. & Btr.	Stud/Gable/Sill/Hdr.	6	EA
2x4 - 10' Std. & Btr.	Stud/Gable	12	EA
3/8" T1-11 Siding	Wall Shthg./Siding	7	EA
5# 16d Galv. Nails	General Framing	1	EA
5# 8d Galv. Nails	General Framing	1	EA
5# 8d Ctd. Box Nails	General Framing	1	EA

CEILING/ROOF

Item	Location	Qty	UM
2x4 - 10' Std. & Btr.	Sub-Fascia	2	EA
2x4 - 10' Std. & Btr.	Rafter/Rake	10	EA
2x6 - 10' Std. & Btr.	Ridge Board	1	EA
2x2 - 10' Std. & Btr.	Soffit Nailer	2	EA
7/16" OSB (Ply.)	Roof Decking	3	EA
1x6 - 8' Std. & Btr.	Fascia	2	EA
1x6 - 10' Std. & Btr.	Fascia	2	EA
3 -Tab Shingles 20 Yr.	Shingle	3	BN
15-lb. Asphalt Rfg. Felt	Roofing	1	RL
1x4 - 8' Std. & Btr. (Rip-1x2)	Soffit Trim	1	EA
Galv. Drip Edge	Fascia	4	EA
5# 8d Ctd. Box Nails	General Framing	2	EA
5# 10d Bright Box Nails	General Framing	2	EA
5# 16d Galv. Nails	General Framing	1	EA
5# 1/2" Galv. Roofing Nails	Roofing Felt	1	EA
5# 1-1/4" Galv. Rfg. Nails	Shingle	2	EA
5# 6d Galv. Box Nails	General Framing	1	EA
5# 6d Galv. Finish Nails	Siding/Soffit	1	EA

EXTERIOR TRIM & ACCESSORIES

Item	Location	Qty	UM
1x4 - 8' Std. & Btr.	Corner Trim	8	EA
1/4" Plywood (Sanded)	Soffit Material	1	EA
1x4 - 10' Std. & Btr. (Rip-1x2)	Window/Door Trim	3	EA
1x6 - 10' Std. & Btr.	Window/Door Trim	5	EA
1x1 - 8' Std. & Btr.	Stop	8	EA
.236x24"x48" Clr. Plexi-Glass	Window/Door	3	EA
1/4"x3/4" Screen Moulding	Window Grid	30	LF
1x4 - 8' Std. & Btr. (Rip-1x2)	Door Frame	1	EA
3/4" Plywood	Door Panel	1	EA
3"x3" Brass Hinge w/Screws	Door	2	EA
2x6 - 8' Treated	Planter	1	EA
2x8 - 8' Treated	Planter	1	EA
4 - 2-1/2" #10 Wood Screws	Planter	2	PK
5# 6d Galv. Finish Nails	Siding/Soffit	4	EA
5# 8d Galv. Finish Nails	Window/Door	1	EA
Construction Adhesive	Window/Door	2	TB

THE VICTORIA

Your little gardener will treasure her very own flower boxes that adorn the exterior of this adorable playhouse. Inside, the playhouse offers lots of space for a complete "play" kitchen, table and chairs. Four windows and a central door give the house light and a real feeling of home. Note the decorative trim and keystone detailing. (Note: Play furniture is not included in the plan.)

Dimensions for this playhouse are 8' X 6'.

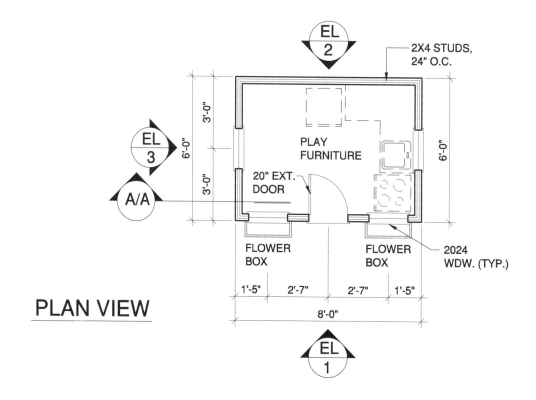

PLAN VIEW

EL 2

2X4 STUDS, 24" O.C.

EL 3

3'-0"

6'-0"

6'-0"

PLAY FURNITURE

A/A

20" EXT. DOOR

3'-0"

FLOWER BOX

FLOWER BOX

2024 WDW. (TYP.)

1'-5" 2'-7" 2'-7" 1'-5"

8'-0"

EL 1

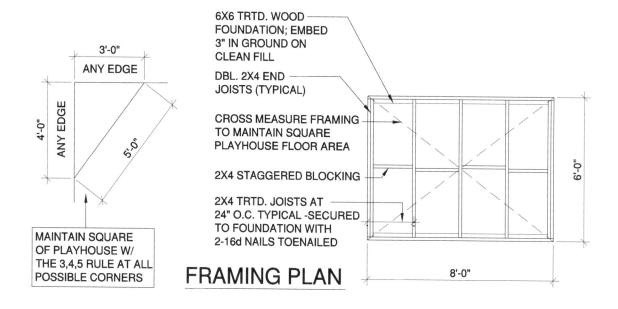

FRAMING PLAN

3'-0"

ANY EDGE

4'-0"

ANY EDGE

5'-0"

MAINTAIN SQUARE OF PLAYHOUSE W/ THE 3,4,5 RULE AT ALL POSSIBLE CORNERS

6X6 TRTD. WOOD FOUNDATION; EMBED 3" IN GROUND ON CLEAN FILL

DBL. 2X4 END JOISTS (TYPICAL)

CROSS MEASURE FRAMING TO MAINTAIN SQUARE PLAYHOUSE FLOOR AREA

2X4 STAGGERED BLOCKING

2X4 TRTD. JOISTS AT 24" O.C. TYPICAL -SECURED TO FOUNDATION WITH 2-16d NAILS TOENAILED

6'-0"

8'-0"

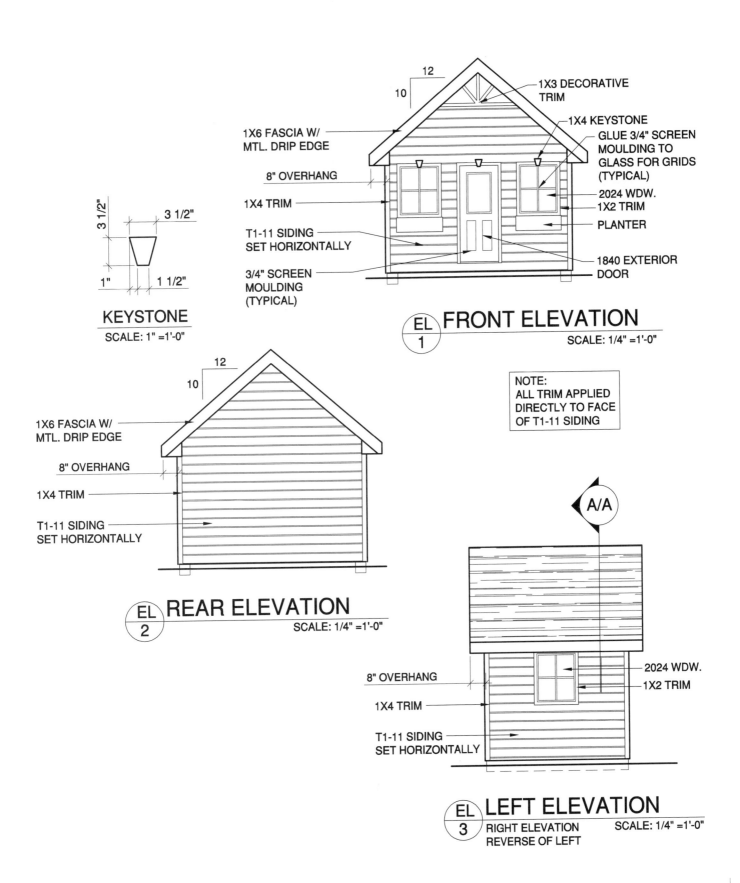

KEYSTONE
SCALE: 1" =1'-0"

3 1/2"
3 1/2"
1"   1 1/2"

1X6 FASCIA W/ MTL. DRIP EDGE

8" OVERHANG

1X4 TRIM

T1-11 SIDING SET HORIZONTALLY

3/4" SCREEN MOULDING (TYPICAL)

12
10

1X3 DECORATIVE TRIM

1X4 KEYSTONE

GLUE 3/4" SCREEN MOULDING TO GLASS FOR GRIDS (TYPICAL)

2024 WDW.
1X2 TRIM

PLANTER

1840 EXTERIOR DOOR

EL 1   FRONT ELEVATION
SCALE: 1/4" =1'-0"

12
10

1X6 FASCIA W/ MTL. DRIP EDGE

8" OVERHANG

1X4 TRIM

T1-11 SIDING SET HORIZONTALLY

EL 2   REAR ELEVATION
SCALE: 1/4" =1'-0"

NOTE:
ALL TRIM APPLIED DIRECTLY TO FACE OF T1-11 SIDING

A/A

8" OVERHANG

1X4 TRIM

T1-11 SIDING SET HORIZONTALLY

2024 WDW.
1X2 TRIM

EL 3   LEFT ELEVATION
RIGHT ELEVATION REVERSE OF LEFT   SCALE: 1/4" =1'-0"

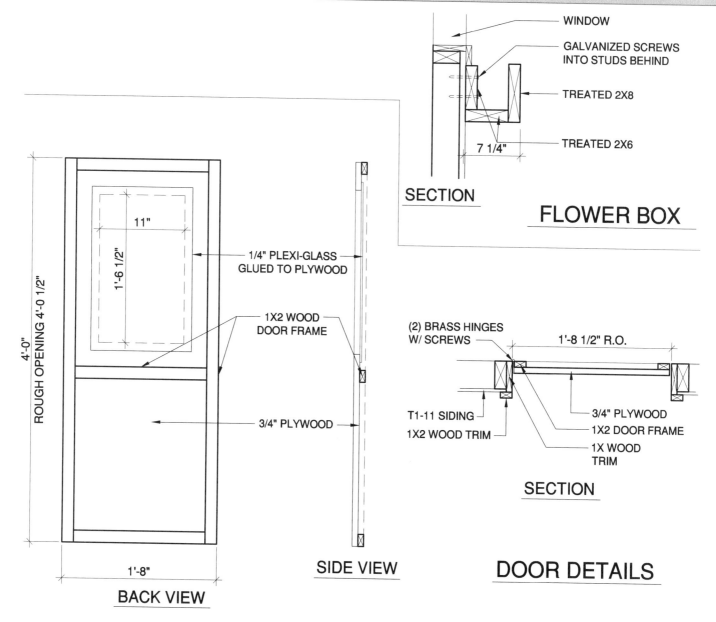

WINDOW

GALVANIZED SCREWS
INTO STUDS BEHIND

TREATED 2X8

7 1/4"

TREATED 2X6

SECTION

FLOWER BOX

11"

1'-6 1/2"

1/4" PLEXI-GLASS
GLUED TO PLYWOOD

ROUGH OPENING 4'-0 1/2"

4'-0"

1X2 WOOD
DOOR FRAME

3/4" PLYWOOD

1'-8"

BACK VIEW

SIDE VIEW

(2) BRASS HINGES
W/ SCREWS

1'-8 1/2" R.O.

T1-11 SIDING

1X2 WOOD TRIM

3/4" PLYWOOD

1X2 DOOR FRAME

1X WOOD
TRIM

SECTION

DOOR DETAILS

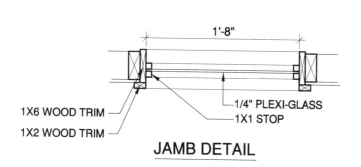

1'-8"

1X6 WOOD TRIM

1X2 WOOD TRIM

1/4" PLEXI-GLASS

1X1 STOP

JAMB DETAIL

WINDOW DETAILS

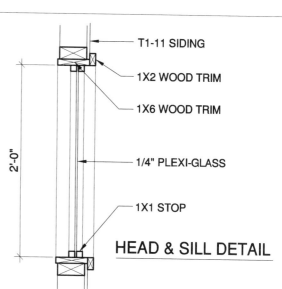

T1-11 SIDING

1X2 WOOD TRIM

1X6 WOOD TRIM

1/4" PLEXI-GLASS

2'-0"

1X1 STOP

HEAD & SILL DETAIL

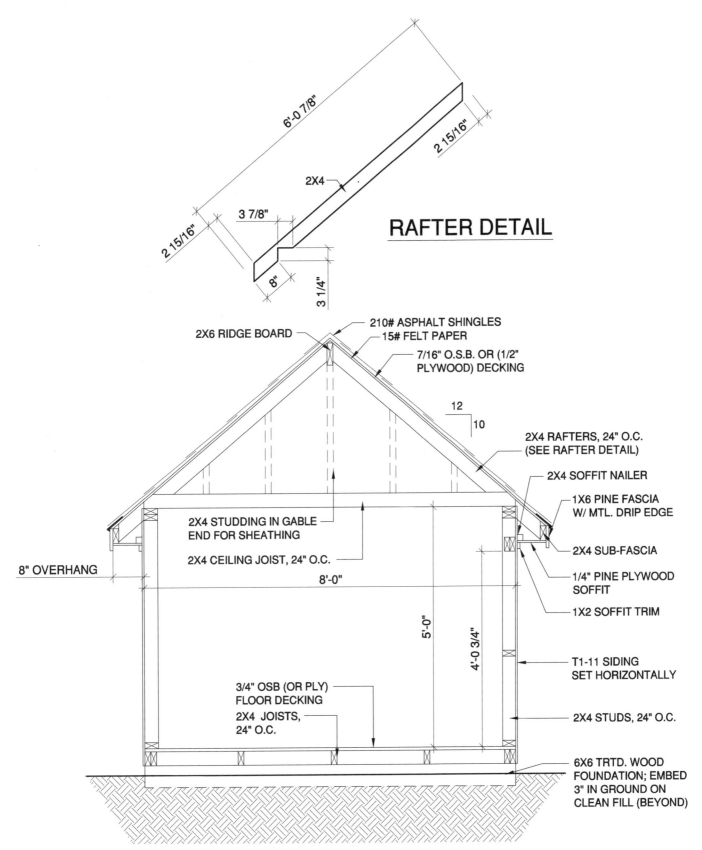

6'-0 7/8"

2 15/16"

2X4

3 7/8"

2 15/16"

8"

3 1/4"

RAFTER DETAIL

2X6 RIDGE BOARD

210# ASPHALT SHINGLES
15# FELT PAPER

7/16" O.S.B. OR (1/2"
PLYWOOD) DECKING

12
10

2X4 RAFTERS, 24" O.C.
(SEE RAFTER DETAIL)

2X4 SOFFIT NAILER

1X6 PINE FASCIA
W/ MTL. DRIP EDGE

2X4 SUB-FASCIA

1/4" PINE PLYWOOD
SOFFIT

1X2 SOFFIT TRIM

2X4 STUDDING IN GABLE
END FOR SHEATHING

2X4 CEILING JOIST, 24" O.C.

8'-0"

8" OVERHANG

5'-0"

4'-0 3/4"

T1-11 SIDING
SET HORIZONTALLY

3/4" OSB (OR PLY)
FLOOR DECKING

2X4 JOISTS,
24" O.C.

2X4 STUDS, 24" O.C.

6X6 TRTD. WOOD
FOUNDATION; EMBED
3" IN GROUND ON
CLEAN FILL (BEYOND)

TYPICAL SECTION

FOUNDATION

Item	Location	Qty	UM
6x6 - 8' Treated	Foundation	2	EA

FLOOR

Item	Location	Qty	UM
2x4 - 8' Treated	Joist/Blocking	4	EA
2x4 - 12' Treated	Joist	3	EA
3/4" OSB (Ply.)	Floor Decking	2	EA
5# 16d Galv. Nails	General Framing	1	EA
5# 8d Ctd. Box Nails	General Framing	1	EA
1# 2-1/2" Ctd. Ext. Screws	Floor Decking	1	EA

WALL FRAMING

Item	Location	Qty	UM
2x4 - 8' Std. & Btr.	Cap/Top/Bottom Plt.	6	EA
2x4 - 12' Std. & Btr.	Cap/Top/Bottom Plt.	3	EA
2x4 - 10' Std. & Btr.	Stud/Gable/Sill/Hdr.	20	EA
3/8" T1-11 Siding	Wall Shthg./Siding	7	EA
5# 16d Galv. Nails	General Framing	1	EA
5# 8d Galv. Nails	General Framing	1	EA
5# 8d Ctd. Box Nails	General Framing	1	EA

CEILING/ROOF

Item	Location	Qty	UM
2x4 - 8' Std. & Btr.	Sub-Fascia/Raft./Clg. Jst.	22	EA
2x6 - 8' Std. & Btr.	Ridge Board	1	EA
2x2 - 12' Std. & Btr.	Soffit Nailer	1	EA
7/16" OSB (Ply.)	Roof Decking	3	EA
1x6 - 8' Std. & Btr.	Fascia	6	EA
3 -Tab Shingles 20 Yr.	Shingle	3	BN
15-lb. Asphalt Rfg. Felt	Roofing	1	RL
1x4 - 8' Std. & Btr. (Rip-1x2)	Soffit Trim	1	EA
Galv. Drip Edge	Fascia	6	EA
5# 8d Ctd. Box Nails	General Framing	2	EA
5# 10d Bright Box Nails	General Framing	2	EA
5# 16d Galv. Nails	General Framing	1	EA
5# 1/2" Galv. Roofing Nails	Roofing Felt	1	EA
5# 1-1/4" Galv. Rfg. Nails	Shingle	2	EA
5# 6d Galv. Box Nails	General Framing	1	EA
5# 6d Galv. Finish Nails	Siding/Soffit	1	EA

EXTERIOR TRIM & ACCESSORIES

Item	Location	Qty	UM
1x4 - 8' Std. & Btr.	Corner Trim/Keystone	8	EA
1/4" Plywood (Sanded)	Soffit Material	2	EA
1x4 - 10' Std. & Btr. (Rip-1x2)	Window/Door Trim	3	EA
1x6 - 10' Std. & Btr.	Window/Door Trim	6	EA
1x1 - 8' Std. & Btr.	Stop	8	EA
.236x24"x48" Clr. Plexi-Glass	Window/Door	3	EA
1/4"x3/4" Screen Moulding	Window Grid	34	LF
1x4 - 8' Std. & Btr. (Rip-1x2)	Door Frame	1	EA
3/4" Plywood	Door Panel	1	EA
3"x3" Brass Hinge w/Screws	Door	2	EA
2x6 - 8' Treated	Planter	2	EA
2x8 - 8' Treated	Planter	1	EA
4 - 2-1/2" #10 Wood Screws	Planter	4	PK
1x3 - 8' Std. & Btr.	Decorative Gable Trim	2	EA
5# 6d Galv. Finish Nails	Siding/Soffit	4	EA
5# 8d Galv. Finish Nails	Window/Door	1	EA
Construction Adhesive	Window/Door	2	TB

THE NASHVILLE

HPM-1500

Three windows and a rustic railed front porch give this playhouse authentic charm. Your child can add curtains to the windows and play furniture to the interior to make it even more homey. The memories created in this playhouse will stay with your family for a lifetime and will be well worth the time and effort you'll invest. (Note: Play furniture is not included in the plan.)

Dimensions for this playhouse are 8' X 6'.

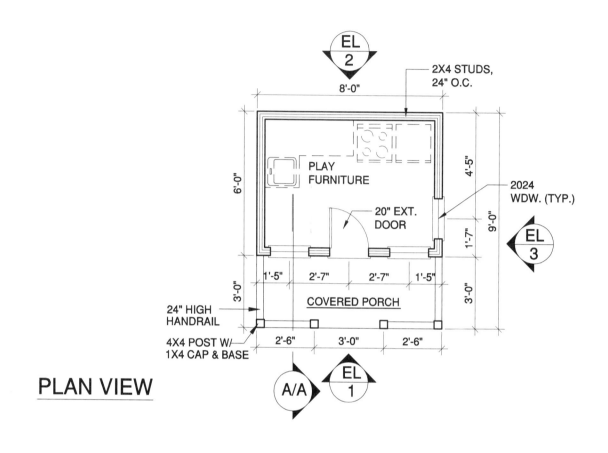

PLAN VIEW

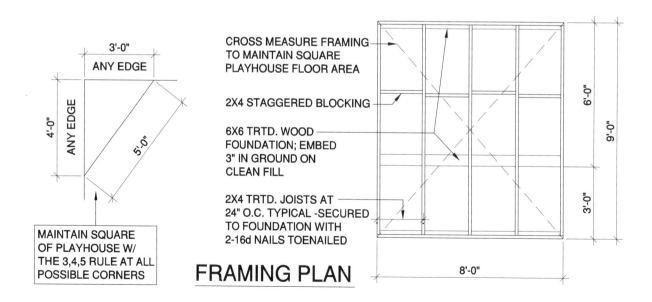

FRAMING PLAN

MAINTAIN SQUARE
OF PLAYHOUSE W/
THE 3,4,5 RULE AT ALL
POSSIBLE CORNERS

CROSS MEASURE FRAMING
TO MAINTAIN SQUARE
PLAYHOUSE FLOOR AREA

2X4 STAGGERED BLOCKING

6X6 TRTD. WOOD
FOUNDATION; EMBED
3" IN GROUND ON
CLEAN FILL

2X4 TRTD. JOISTS AT
24" O.C. TYPICAL -SECURED
TO FOUNDATION WITH
2-16d NAILS TOENAILED

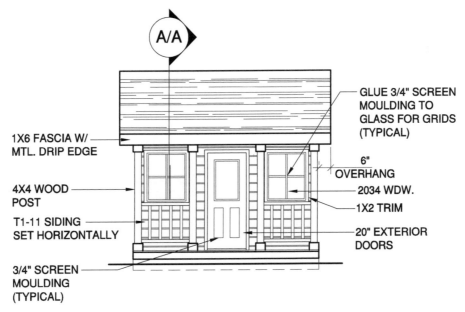

GLUE 3/4" SCREEN
MOULDING TO
GLASS FOR GRIDS
(TYPICAL)

1X6 FASCIA W/
MTL. DRIP EDGE

6"
OVERHANG

4X4 WOOD
POST

2034 WDW.

1X2 TRIM

T1-11 SIDING
SET HORIZONTALLY

20" EXTERIOR
DOORS

3/4" SCREEN
MOULDING
(TYPICAL)

EL 1 FRONT ELEVATION

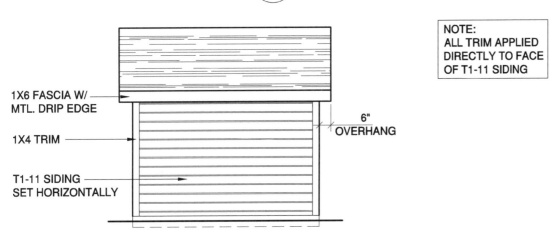

1X6 FASCIA W/
MTL. DRIP EDGE

1X4 TRIM

T1-11 SIDING
SET HORIZONTALLY

6"
OVERHANG

NOTE:
ALL TRIM APPLIED
DIRECTLY TO FACE
OF T1-11 SIDING

EL 2 REAR ELEVATION

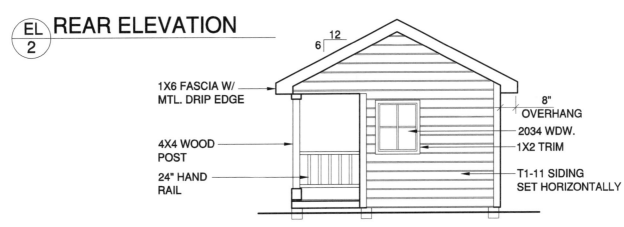

1X6 FASCIA W/
MTL. DRIP EDGE

6 | 12

4X4 WOOD
POST

24" HAND
RAIL

8"
OVERHANG

2034 WDW.

1X2 TRIM

T1-11 SIDING
SET HORIZONTALLY

EL 3 RIGHT ELEVATION
LEFT ELEVATION REVERSE
OF RIGHT WITHOUT WINDOW

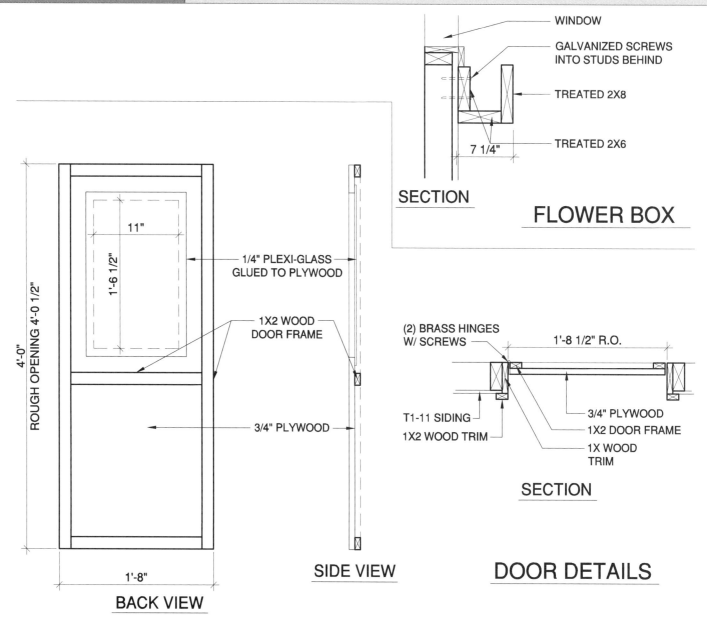

BACK VIEW

11"

1'-6 1/2"

1/4" PLEXI-GLASS GLUED TO PLYWOOD

1X2 WOOD DOOR FRAME

3/4" PLYWOOD

ROUGH OPENING 4'-0 1/2"

4'-0"

1'-8"

SIDE VIEW

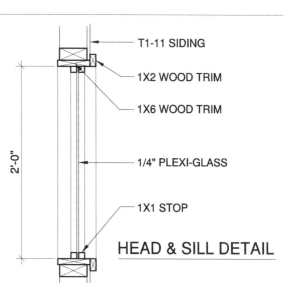

FLOWER BOX

WINDOW

GALVANIZED SCREWS INTO STUDS BEHIND

TREATED 2X8

TREATED 2X6

7 1/4"

SECTION

DOOR DETAILS

(2) BRASS HINGES W/ SCREWS

1'-8 1/2" R.O.

T1-11 SIDING

1X2 WOOD TRIM

3/4" PLYWOOD

1X2 DOOR FRAME

1X WOOD TRIM

SECTION

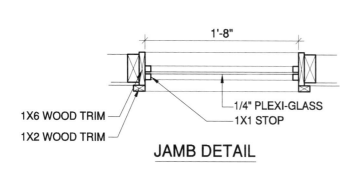

WINDOW DETAILS

1'-8"

1X6 WOOD TRIM

1X2 WOOD TRIM

1/4" PLEXI-GLASS

1X1 STOP

JAMB DETAIL

HEAD & SILL DETAIL

T1-11 SIDING

1X2 WOOD TRIM

1X6 WOOD TRIM

1/4" PLEXI-GLASS

1X1 STOP

2'-0"

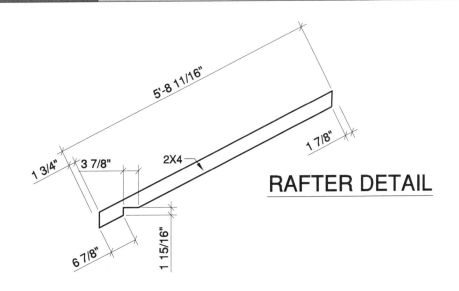

RAFTER DETAIL

5'-8 11/16"

1 3/4" 3 7/8" 2X4 1 7/8"

6 7/8" 1 15/16"

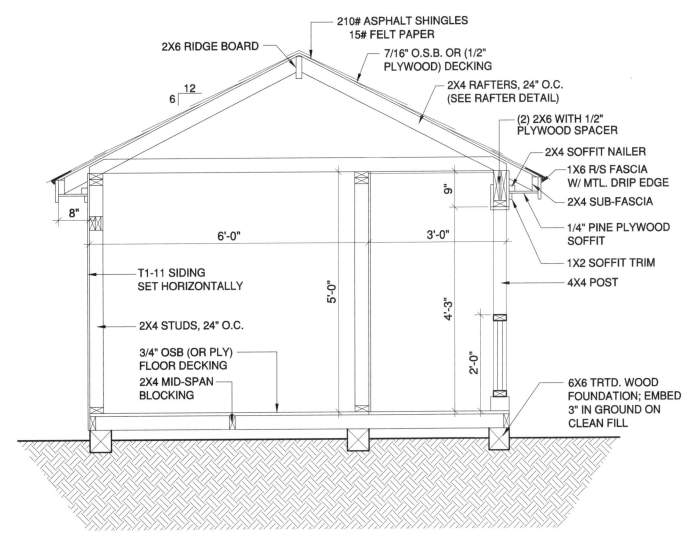

210# ASPHALT SHINGLES
15# FELT PAPER

2X6 RIDGE BOARD

7/16" O.S.B. OR (1/2"
PLYWOOD) DECKING

2X4 RAFTERS, 24" O.C.
(SEE RAFTER DETAIL)

6 | 12

(2) 2X6 WITH 1/2"
PLYWOOD SPACER

2X4 SOFFIT NAILER

1X6 R/S FASCIA
W/ MTL. DRIP EDGE

2X4 SUB-FASCIA

1/4" PINE PLYWOOD
SOFFIT

1X2 SOFFIT TRIM

4X4 POST

8"

9"

6'-0" 3'-0"

5'-0" 4'-3"

T1-11 SIDING
SET HORIZONTALLY

2X4 STUDS, 24" O.C.

3/4" OSB (OR PLY)
FLOOR DECKING

2X4 MID-SPAN
BLOCKING

2'-0"

6X6 TRTD. WOOD
FOUNDATION; EMBED
3" IN GROUND ON
CLEAN FILL

A/A SECTION

FOUNDATION

Item	Location	Qty	UM
6x6 - 8' Treated	Foundation	3	EA

FLOOR

Item	Location	Qty	UM
2x4 - 8' Treated	Joist/Blocking	3	EA
2x4 - 10' Treated	Joist	5	EA
3/4" OSB (Ply.)	Floor Decking	3	EA
5# 16d Galv. Nails	General Framing	1	EA
5# 8d Ctd. Box Nails	General Framing	1	EA
1# 2-1/2" Ctd. Ext. Screws	Floor Decking	1	EA

WALL FRAMING

Item	Location	Qty	UM
2x4 - 8' Std. & Btr.	Cap/Top/Bottom Plt.	6	EA
2x4 - 12' Std. & Btr.	Cap/Top/Bottom Plt.	3	EA
2x4 - 10' Std. & Btr.	Stud/Gable/Sill/Hdr.	18	EA
3/8" T1-11 Siding	Wall Shthg./Siding	7	EA
5# 16d Galv. Nails	General Framing	1	EA
5# 8d Galv. Nails	General Framing	1	EA
5# 8d Ctd. Box Nails	General Framing	1	EA

CEILING/ROOF

Item	Location	Qty	UM
2x4 - 10' Std. & Btr.	Sub-Fascia/Clg. Jst.	7	EA
2x4 - 12' Std. & Btr.	Rafter	5	EA
2x6 - 10' Std. & Btr.	Ridge Board	1	EA
2x2 - 8' Std. & Btr.	Soffit Nailer	2	EA
7/16" OSB (Ply.)	Roof Decking	4	EA
1x6 - 10' Std. & Btr.	Fascia	2	EA
1x6 - 12' Std. & Btr.	Fascia	2	EA
3 -Tab Shingles 20 Yr.	Shingle	4	BN
15-lb. Asphalt Rfg. Felt	Roofing	1	RL
1x4 - 8' Std. & Btr. (Rip-1x2)	Soffit Trim	3	EA
Galv. Drip Edge	Fascia	5	EA
5# 8d Ctd. Box Nails	General Framing	2	EA
5# 10d Bright Box Nails	General Framing	2	EA
5# 16d Galv. Nails	General Framing	1	EA
5# 1/2" Galv. Roofing Nails	Roofing Felt	1	EA
5# 1-1/4" Galv. Rfg. Nails	Shingle	2	EA
5# 6d Galv. Box Nails	General Framing	1	EA
5# 6d Galv. Finish Nails	Siding/Soffit	1	EA

EXTERIOR TRIM & ACCESSORIES

Item	Location	Qty	UM
4x4 - 10' Treated	Porch Post	4	EA
2x6 - 8' Std. & Btr.	Porch Beam	2	EA
1/2" CDX - 5 Ply Plywd.	Beam Spacer	1	EA
2x4 - 8' Std. & Btr.	Beam Nailer Plate	1	EA
1x4 - 8' Std. & Btr.	Post Trim	2	EA
1x6 - 8' Std. & Btr.	Beam Wrap	1	EA
1x8 - 8' Std. & Btr.	Beam Wrap	2	EA
2x4 - 12' Std. & Btr.	Cap/Bottom Rail	2	EA
2"x2" - 4' Sq. Baluster	Baluster	10	EA
1x4 - 8' Std. & Btr.	Corner Trim	8	EA
1/4" Plywood (Sanded)	Soffit Material	2	EA
1x4 - 10' Std. & Btr. (Rip-1x2)	Window/Door Trim	3	EA
1x6 - 10' Std. & Btr.	Window/Door Trim	5	EA
1x1 - 8' Std. & Btr.	Stop	6	EA
.236x24"x48" Clr. Plexi-Glass	Window/Door	2	EA
1/4"x3/4" Screen Moulding	Window Grid	26	LF
1x4 - 8' Std. & Btr. (Rip-1x2)	Door Frame	1	EA
3/4" Plywood	Door Panel	1	EA
3"x3" Brass Hinge w/Screws	Door	2	EA
5# 6d Galv. Finish Nails	Siding/Soffit	4	EA
5# 8d Galv. Finish Nails	Window/Door	1	EA
Construction Adhesive	Window/Door	2	TB

THE CASTLETON

HPM-1703

Attractive and durable, this unique sandbox will entertain the kids for hours, and at the same time it will keep your yard looking neat and clean. Supervising adults will enjoy the handy benches built into two of its corners. This simple, do-it-yourself project can be built to complement your other yard accessories.

Dimensions for this sandbox are 14' X 14'.

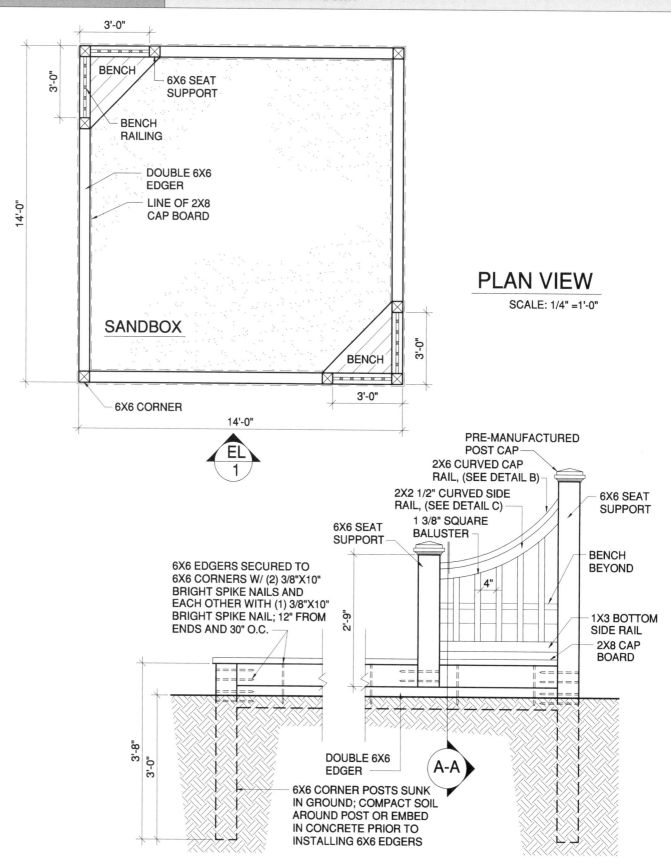

PLAN VIEW

SCALE: 1/4" =1'-0"

3'-0"

3'-0"

BENCH

6X6 SEAT SUPPORT

BENCH RAILING

DOUBLE 6X6 EDGER

LINE OF 2X8 CAP BOARD

14'-0"

SANDBOX

BENCH

3'-0"

6X6 CORNER

14'-0"

3'-0"

EL 1

PRE-MANUFACTURED POST CAP

2X6 CURVED CAP RAIL, (SEE DETAIL B)

2X2 1/2" CURVED SIDE RAIL, (SEE DETAIL C)

1 3/8" SQUARE BALUSTER

6X6 SEAT SUPPORT

6X6 SEAT SUPPORT

BENCH BEYOND

4"

1X3 BOTTOM SIDE RAIL

2X8 CAP BOARD

6X6 EDGERS SECURED TO 6X6 CORNERS W/ (2) 3/8"X10" BRIGHT SPIKE NAILS AND EACH OTHER WITH (1) 3/8"X10" BRIGHT SPIKE NAIL; 12" FROM ENDS AND 30" O.C.

2'-9"

3'-8"

3'-0"

DOUBLE 6X6 EDGER

6X6 CORNER POSTS SUNK IN GROUND; COMPACT SOIL AROUND POST OR EMBED IN CONCRETE PRIOR TO INSTALLING 6X6 EDGERS

A-A

TYPICAL DETAIL

SCALE: 1/2" =1'-0"

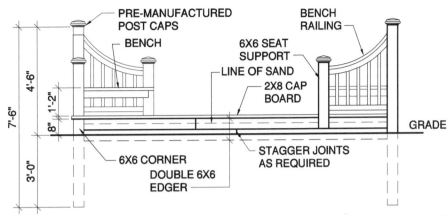

PRE-MANUFACTURED
POST CAPS

BENCH
RAILING

BENCH

6X6 SEAT
SUPPORT

LINE OF SAND

2X8 CAP
BOARD

GRADE

6X6 CORNER

DOUBLE 6X6
EDGER

STAGGER JOINTS
AS REQUIRED

4'-6"
1'-2"
8"
3'-0"
7'-6"

FRONT ELEVATION

EL 1

SCALE: 1/4" =1'-0"
OTHER ELEVATIONS SIMILAR

2X6 CURVED CAP
RAIL, (SEE DETAIL)

2X2 1/2" CURVED SIDE
RAIL, (SEE DETAIL)

2X BLKG. BETWEEN
BALUSTERS, TYP.

1 3/8" SQUARE
BALUSTER

6X6 SEAT SUPPORT
BEYOND

2X6 SEAT SLATS

2X4 SEAT FRAMING

1X3 BOTTOM RAIL

2X8 CAP BOARD

DOUBLE 6X6
EDGER

3/8"X10" BRIGHT
SPIKE NAIL

4" TO 6" SAND BED

6 MIL POLY LINER WRAPPED
ONTO EDGER ABOVE JOINT

GRADE

9"
2"
1'-6 1/2"
3"

SECTION

A-A

SCALE: 1" =1'-0"

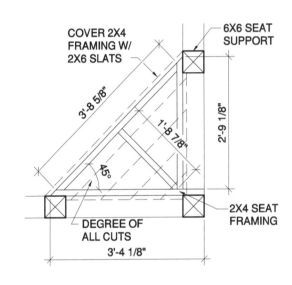

COVER 2X4
FRAMING W/
2X6 SLATS

6X6 SEAT
SUPPORT

3'-8 5/8"
1'-8 7/8"
2'-9 1/8"
45°
DEGREE OF
ALL CUTS
3'-4 1/8"

2X4 SEAT
FRAMING

BENCH FRAMING

SCALE: 1/2" =1'-0"

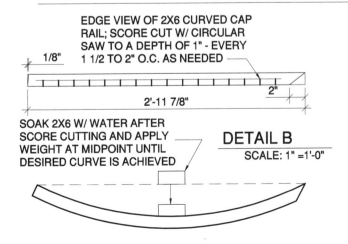

EDGE VIEW OF 2X6 CURVED CAP
RAIL; SCORE CUT W/ CIRCULAR
SAW TO A DEPTH OF 1" - EVERY
1 1/2 TO 2" O.C. AS NEEDED

1/8"
2'-11 7/8"
2"

SOAK 2X6 W/ WATER AFTER
SCORE CUTTING AND APPLY
WEIGHT AT MIDPOINT UNTIL
DESIRED CURVE IS ACHIEVED

DETAIL B

SCALE: 1" =1'-0"

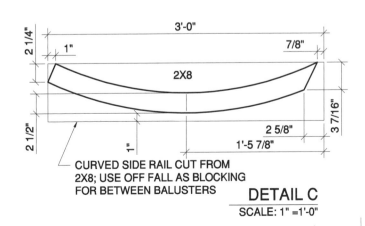

3'-0"
2 1/4"
1"
7/8"
2X8
2 1/2"
3 7/16"
1"
2 5/8"
1'-5 7/8"

CURVED SIDE RAIL CUT FROM
2X8; USE OFF FALL AS BLOCKING
FOR BETWEEN BALUSTERS

DETAIL C

SCALE: 1" =1'-0"

FOUNDATION

Item	Location	Qty	UM
6x6 - 8' Treated	Edger/Corner Post	19	EA
2x8 - 16' Treated	Edger Cap Plate	4	EA
6 Mil Poly Sheeting	Box Bottom	1	RL
50# 3/8"x10" Bright Spike	Edger/Post	1	EA
5# 16d Galv. Nails	General Framing	1	EA
5# 10d Galv. Nails	General Framing	1	EA
5# 8d Galv. Nails	General Framing	1	EA

FRAMING/BENCH/SEAT

Item	Location	Qty	UM
6x6 - 8' Treated	Seat Support Post	2	EA
2x4 - 12' Treated	Seat Framing	2	EA
2x6 - 16' Treated	Seat Slat	2	EA

FINISH/RAILING

Item	Location	Qty	UM
2x6 - 8' Treated	Top Rail	2	EA
2x8 - 8' Treated	Top Side Rail	4	EA
1x3 - 8' Treated	Bottom Side Rail	4	EA
2x3 - 8' Treated	Baluster Blocking	3	EA
1-3/8"x1-3/8" - 3' Sq. Blstr.	Baluster	21	EA
Wood Post Cap	Post	8	EA

THE CANINE CASTLE

HPM-1700

Your dog will be the king of the neighborhood in his very own castle! Wood shakes on the roof keep your furry friend dry and protected from the outdoor elements. The spacious 4'x5' interior leaves plenty of room for your pet to turn around or curl up, and still keep an eye on the yard!

Dimensions for this doghouse are 4' X 5'.

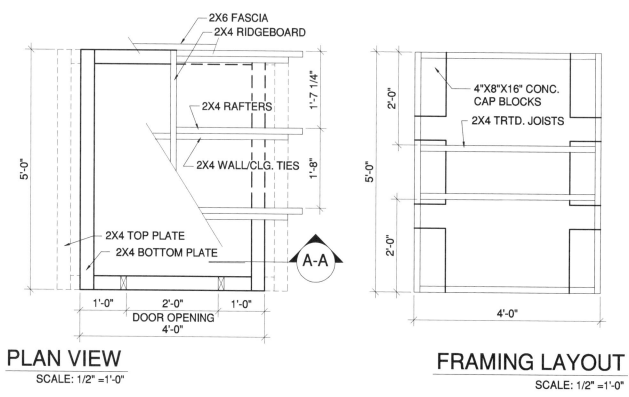

PLAN VIEW
SCALE: 1/2" =1'-0"

2X6 FASCIA
2X4 RIDGEBOARD
2X4 RAFTERS
2X4 WALL/CLG. TIES
2X4 TOP PLATE
2X4 BOTTOM PLATE
A-A

1'-7 1/4"
1'-8"
5'-0"

1'-0"   2'-0"   1'-0"
DOOR OPENING
4'-0"

FRAMING LAYOUT
SCALE: 1/2" =1'-0"

4"X8"X16" CONC. CAP BLOCKS
2X4 TRTD. JOISTS

2'-0"
5'-0"
2'-0"

4'-0"

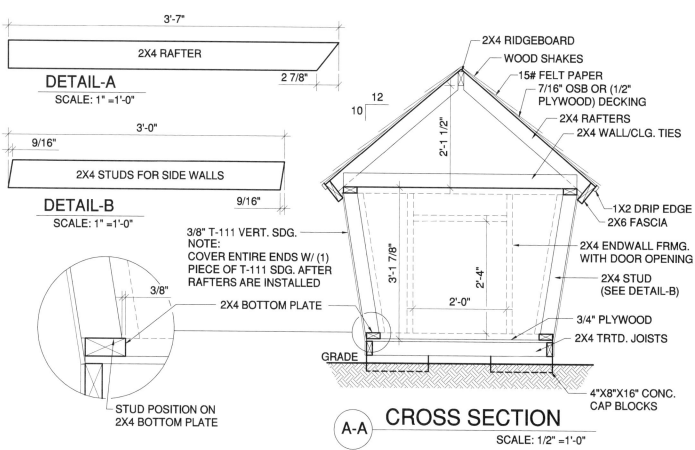

DETAIL-A
SCALE: 1" =1'-0"

3'-7"
2X4 RAFTER
2 7/8"

DETAIL-B
SCALE: 1" =1'-0"

3'-0"
9/16"
2X4 STUDS FOR SIDE WALLS
9/16"

3/8"
3/8" T-111 VERT. SDG.
NOTE:
COVER ENTIRE ENDS W/ (1)
PIECE OF T-111 SDG. AFTER
RAFTERS ARE INSTALLED
2X4 BOTTOM PLATE

STUD POSITION ON
2X4 BOTTOM PLATE

CROSS SECTION
A-A
SCALE: 1/2" =1'-0"

2X4 RIDGEBOARD
WOOD SHAKES
15# FELT PAPER
7/16" OSB OR (1/2" PLYWOOD) DECKING
2X4 RAFTERS
2X4 WALL/CLG. TIES
1X2 DRIP EDGE
2X6 FASCIA
2X4 ENDWALL FRMG. WITH DOOR OPENING
2X4 STUD (SEE DETAIL-B)
3/4" PLYWOOD
2X4 TRTD. JOISTS
4"X8"X16" CONC. CAP BLOCKS
GRADE

10 | 12
2'-1 1/2"
3'-1 7/8"
2'-4"
2'-0"

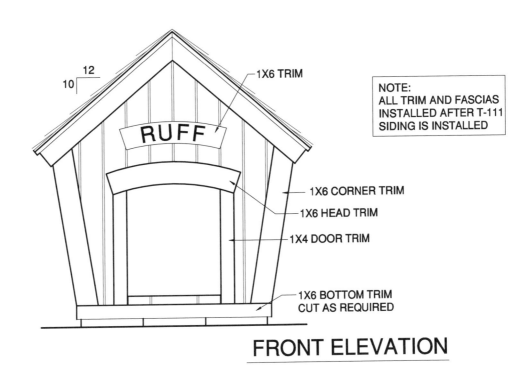

12
10

1X6 TRIM

RUFF

NOTE:
ALL TRIM AND FASCIAS
INSTALLED AFTER T-111
SIDING IS INSTALLED

1X6 CORNER TRIM

1X6 HEAD TRIM

1X4 DOOR TRIM

1X6 BOTTOM TRIM
CUT AS REQUIRED

FRONT ELEVATION

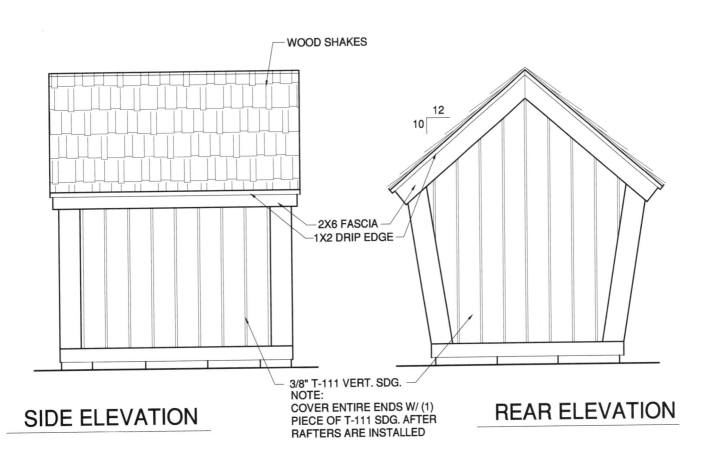

WOOD SHAKES

2X6 FASCIA
1X2 DRIP EDGE

12
10

3/8" T-111 VERT. SDG.
NOTE:
COVER ENTIRE ENDS W/ (1)
PIECE OF T-111 SDG. AFTER
RAFTERS ARE INSTALLED

SIDE ELEVATION

REAR ELEVATION

FOUNDATION

Item	Location	Qty	UM
4"x8"x16" Conc. Cap Blk.	Foundation	6	EA

WALL

Item	Location	Qty	UM
2x4 - 8' Treated	Joist	2	EA
2x4 - 10' Treated	Joist	1	EA
3/4" OSB (Ply.)	Floor Decking	1	EA
2x4 - 8' Std. & Btr.	Bottom Plate	1	EA
2x4 - 10' Std. & Btr.	Bottom/Top Plate	3	EA
2x4 - 12' Std. & Btr.	Side/End Stud	4	EA
5# 16d Galv. Nails	General Framing	1	EA
5# 8d Galv. Nails	General Framing	1	EA

ROOF

Item	Location	Qty	UM
2x4 - 8' Std. & Btr.	Rafter/Ridge Board/Door Hdr.	5	EA
2x4 - 12' Std. & Btr.	Wall - Ceiling Tie	2	EA
7/16" OSB (Ply.)	Roof Decking	2	EA
15-lb. Asphalt Rfg. Felt	Roof	1	RL
Wood Shake	Roof	48	SF
Wood Ridge Shake	Ridge	6	LF
1# 8d Ring Shank Nails	Shake	3	EA
5# 16d Galv. Nails	General Framing	1	EA
5# 8d Galv. Nails	General Framing	1	EA
5# 8d Coated Box Nails	Finish Framing	1	EA

FINISH/TRIM

Item	Location	Qty	UM
1x2 - 8' Std. & Btr.	Drip Edge	2	EA
1x2 - 12' Std. & Btr.	Drip Edge	1	EA
1x4 - 8' Std. & Btr.	Door Trim	1	EA
1x6 - 8' Std. & Btr.	Corner/Dr. Trim/Name Plate	5	EA
1x6 - 10' Std. & Btr.	Bottom Trim	2	EA
2x6 - 8' Std. & Btr.	Fascia	2	EA
2x6 - 12' Std. & Btr.	Fascia	1	EA
3/8" T1-11 Vert. Siding	Siding	3	EA
5# 8d Coated Box Nails	Finish Framing	1	EA

THE DRAWBRIDGE

HPM-1702

Enjoy the charm of a bubbling creek in your backyard with this enchanting bridge. Whether you actually have water flowing beneath it, or a colorful garden bed, the drama created by this bridge will be spectacular. Using different design elements, you can adapt the bridge and your surrounding landscape to the changing seasons and holidays.

Dimensions for this bridge are 5' X 24'.

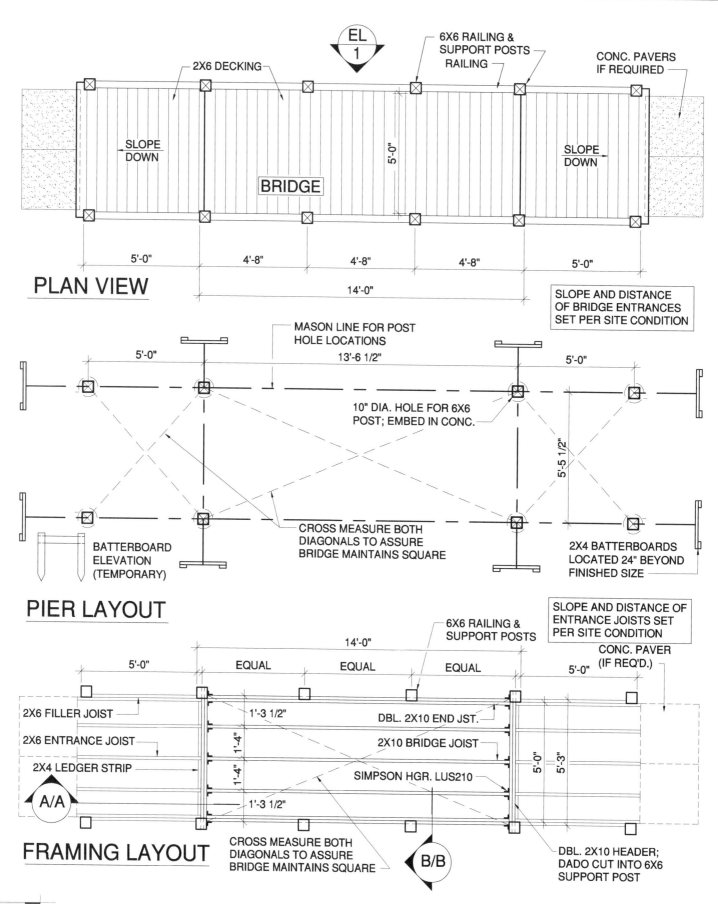

PLAN VIEW

EL 1

2X6 DECKING
6X6 RAILING & SUPPORT POSTS RAILING
CONC. PAVERS IF REQUIRED
SLOPE DOWN
SLOPE DOWN
5'-0"
BRIDGE

5'-0" | 4'-8" | 4'-8" | 4'-8" | 5'-0"
14'-0"

SLOPE AND DISTANCE OF BRIDGE ENTRANCES SET PER SITE CONDITION

PIER LAYOUT

MASON LINE FOR POST HOLE LOCATIONS
5'-0"
13'-6 1/2"
5'-0"
10" DIA. HOLE FOR 6X6 POST; EMBED IN CONC.
5'-5 1/2"
BATTERBOARD ELEVATION (TEMPORARY)
CROSS MEASURE BOTH DIAGONALS TO ASSURE BRIDGE MAINTAINS SQUARE
2X4 BATTERBOARDS LOCATED 24" BEYOND FINISHED SIZE

FRAMING LAYOUT

SLOPE AND DISTANCE OF ENTRANCE JOISTS SET PER SITE CONDITION
6X6 RAILING & SUPPORT POSTS
CONC. PAVER (IF REQ'D.)
14'-0"
5'-0" | EQUAL | EQUAL | EQUAL | 5'-0"
2X6 FILLER JOIST
1'-3 1/2"
DBL. 2X10 END JST.
2X6 ENTRANCE JOIST
1'-4"
2X10 BRIDGE JOIST
2X4 LEDGER STRIP
1'-4"
SIMPSON HGR. LUS210
5'-0"
5'-3"
A/A
1'-3 1/2"
CROSS MEASURE BOTH DIAGONALS TO ASSURE BRIDGE MAINTAINS SQUARE
B/B
DBL. 2X10 HEADER; DADO CUT INTO 6X6 SUPPORT POST

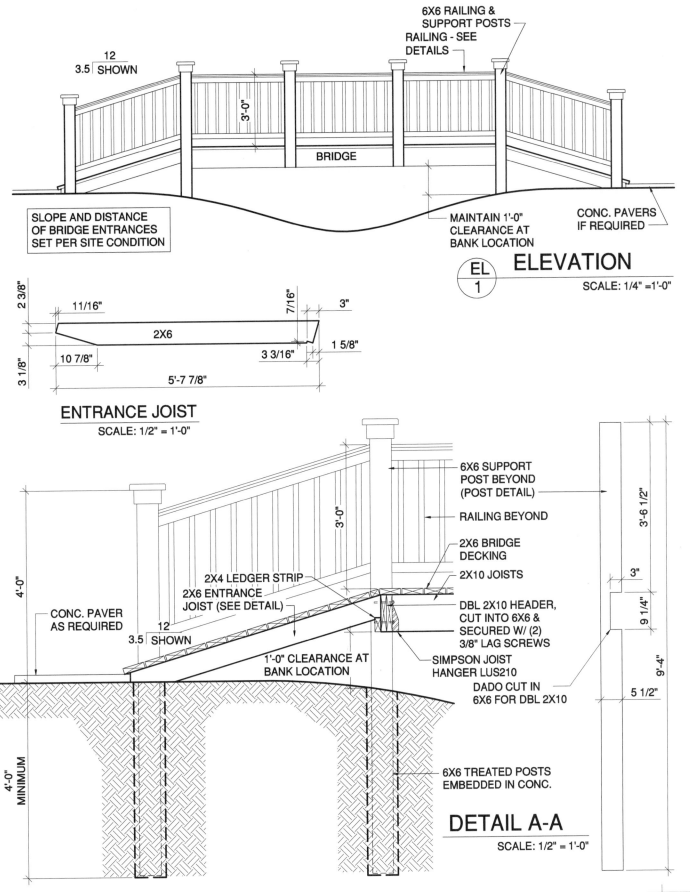

ELEVATION

6X6 RAILING & SUPPORT POSTS RAILING - SEE DETAILS

12 / 3.5 SHOWN

3'-0"

BRIDGE

SLOPE AND DISTANCE OF BRIDGE ENTRANCES SET PER SITE CONDITION

MAINTAIN 1'-0" CLEARANCE AT BANK LOCATION

CONC. PAVERS IF REQUIRED

EL 1

SCALE: 1/4" =1'-0"

ENTRANCE JOIST

2 3/8"
11/16"
7/16"
3"
2X6
3 1/8"
10 7/8"
3 3/16"
1 5/8"
5'-7 7/8"

SCALE: 1/2" = 1'-0"

DETAIL A-A

6X6 SUPPORT POST BEYOND (POST DETAIL)

RAILING BEYOND

2X6 BRIDGE DECKING

2X10 JOISTS

2X4 LEDGER STRIP

2X6 ENTRANCE JOIST (SEE DETAIL)

DBL 2X10 HEADER, CUT INTO 6X6 & SECURED W/ (2) 3/8" LAG SCREWS

SIMPSON JOIST HANGER LUS210

DADO CUT IN 6X6 FOR DBL 2X10

1'-0" CLEARANCE AT BANK LOCATION

3'-0"

12 / 3.5 SHOWN

4'-0"

CONC. PAVER AS REQUIRED

4'-0" MINIMUM

6X6 TREATED POSTS EMBEDDED IN CONC.

3'-6 1/2"

3"

9 1/4"

9'-4"

5 1/2"

SCALE: 1/2" = 1'-0"

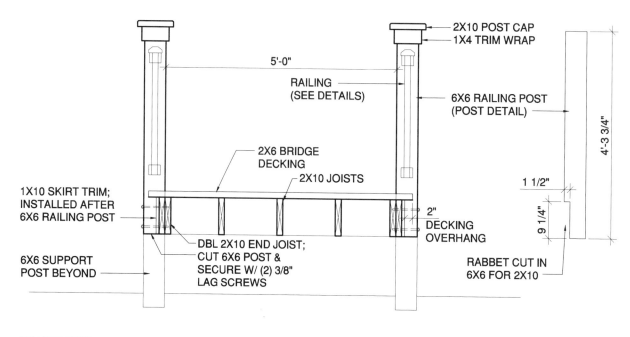

2X10 POST CAP
1X4 TRIM WRAP

5'-0"

RAILING
(SEE DETAILS)

6X6 RAILING POST
(POST DETAIL)

2X6 BRIDGE
DECKING

2X10 JOISTS

1X10 SKIRT TRIM;
INSTALLED AFTER
6X6 RAILING POST

1 1/2"

2"
DECKING
OVERHANG

4'-3 3/4"

9 1/4"

DBL 2X10 END JOIST;
CUT 6X6 POST &
SECURE W/ (2) 3/8"
LAG SCREWS

6X6 SUPPORT
POST BEYOND

RABBET CUT IN
6X6 FOR 2X10

GRADE LINES

DETAIL B-B
SCALE: 1/2" = 1'-0"

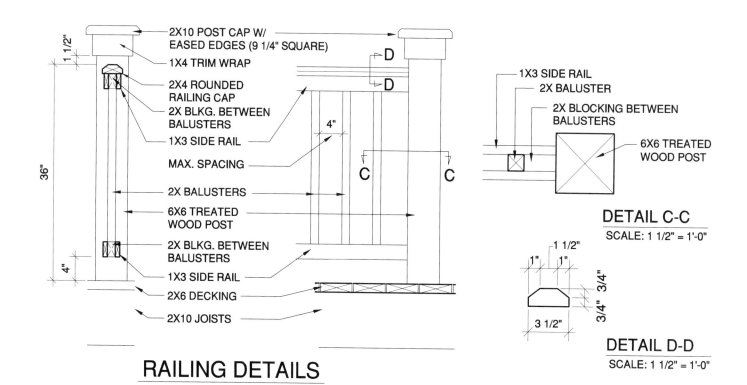

1 1/2"

2X10 POST CAP W/
EASED EDGES (9 1/4" SQUARE)

1X4 TRIM WRAP

2X4 ROUNDED
RAILING CAP

2X BLKG. BETWEEN
BALUSTERS

1X3 SIDE RAIL

D

D

4"

MAX. SPACING

36"

2X BALUSTERS

6X6 TREATED
WOOD POST

C

C

2X BLKG. BETWEEN
BALUSTERS

4"

1X3 SIDE RAIL

2X6 DECKING

2X10 JOISTS

1X3 SIDE RAIL
2X BALUSTER

2X BLOCKING BETWEEN
BALUSTERS

6X6 TREATED
WOOD POST

DETAIL C-C
SCALE: 1 1/2" = 1'-0"

1 1/2"
1"   1"
3/4"
3/4"
3 1/2"

DETAIL D-D
SCALE: 1 1/2" = 1'-0"

RAILING DETAILS
SCALE: 3/4" = 1'-0"

FOUNDATION

Item	Location	Qty	UM
60# Concrete Mix	Post	16	BG
6x6 - 10' Treated	Post	4	EA
6x6 - 8' Treated	Post	4	EA
2x4 - 10' Std. & Btr.	Batterboard	5	EA
5# 16d Galv. Nails	General Framing	3	EA
5# 10d Galv. Nails	General Framing	5	EA
5# 8d Galv. Nails	General Framing	5	EA
5# 8d Coated Box Nails	General Framing	2	EA

FRAMING

Item	Location	Qty	UM
2x10 - 12' Treated	Beam	2	EA
2x10 - 14' Treated	Joist	7	EA
2x6 - 12' Treated	Entrance/Filler Jst.	7	EA
2x4 - 12' Treated	Ledger	1	EA
2x10 Jst. Hngr. (LUS210)	Joist	6	EA
2x10 Jst. Hngr. (LUS210-2)	Joist	4	EA
2x6 - 12' Treated	Decking	31	EA
3/8"x5" Lag Screws	Beam	8	EA
3/8"x6" Lag Screws	Post	8	EA
3/8"x1-1/2" Washer	Post/Beam	16	EA
1# 8d 1-1/2" Jst. Hngr. Nails	Connector	3	EA

FINISH/RAILING/SKIRT

Item	Location	Qty	UM
6x6 - 10' Treated	Post	2	EA
2x4 - 10' Treated	Cap Rail	3	EA
2x4 - 8' Treated	Cap Rail	2	EA
1x3 - 8' Treated	Side Rail	8	EA
1x3 - 10' Treated	Side Rail	12	EA
1x4 - 8' Treated	Post Trim	6	EA
2x3 - 8' Treated	Baluster Blocking	4	EA
2x3 - 10' Treated	Baluster Blocking	6	EA
2"x2" - 3' Sq. Blstr.	Baluster	100	EA
1x10 - 14' Treated	Skirt	2	EA
2x10 - 12' Treated	Post Cap	1	EA
5# 8d Coated Box Nails	Finish Framing	1	EA
1# 2-1/2" Coated Screws	Decking & Railing	8	EA

THE MAYBERRY

HPM-1715

Why not distinguish your mailbox from the rest with this stylish design? Coordinate the wood or the finish to match your home and create a terrific curb appeal at the same time. This easy-to-build mailbox has a sturdy 4x4 base.

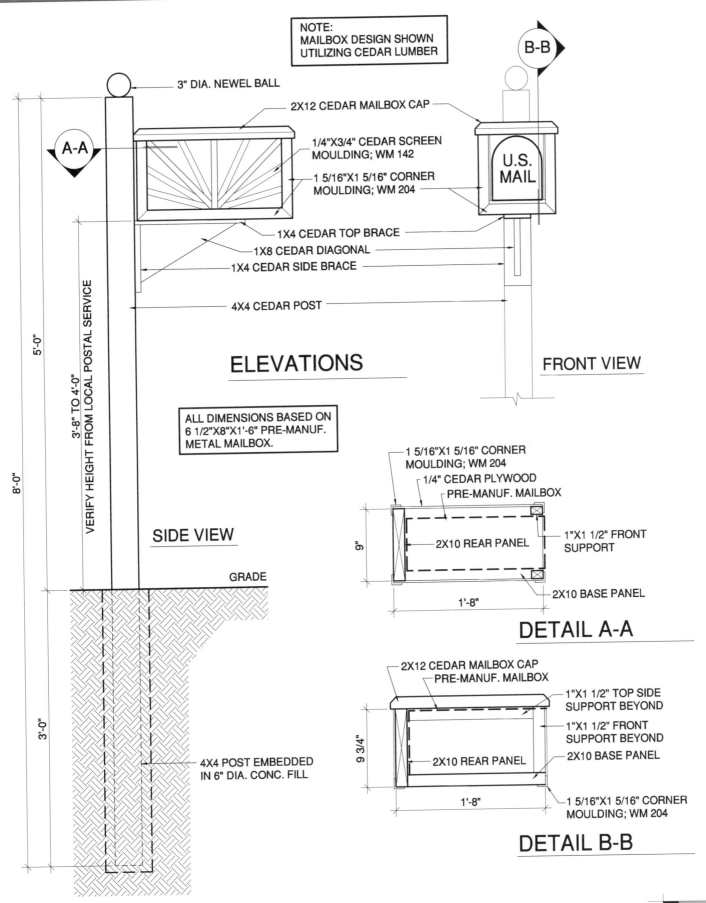

NOTE:
MAILBOX DESIGN SHOWN
UTILIZING CEDAR LUMBER

3" DIA. NEWEL BALL

2X12 CEDAR MAILBOX CAP

1/4"X3/4" CEDAR SCREEN
MOULDING; WM 142

1 5/16"X1 5/16" CORNER
MOULDING; WM 204

U.S. MAIL

1X4 CEDAR TOP BRACE
1X8 CEDAR DIAGONAL
1X4 CEDAR SIDE BRACE

4X4 CEDAR POST

A-A

B-B

ELEVATIONS

FRONT VIEW

5'-0"

3'-8" TO 4'-0"

VERIFY HEIGHT FROM LOCAL POSTAL SERVICE

8'-0"

ALL DIMENSIONS BASED ON
6 1/2"X8"X1'-6" PRE-MANUF.
METAL MAILBOX.

SIDE VIEW

GRADE

3'-0"

4X4 POST EMBEDDED
IN 6" DIA. CONC. FILL

1 5/16"X1 5/16" CORNER
MOULDING; WM 204

1/4" CEDAR PLYWOOD

PRE-MANUF. MAILBOX

9"

2X10 REAR PANEL

1"X1 1/2" FRONT
SUPPORT

2X10 BASE PANEL

1'-8"

DETAIL A-A

2X12 CEDAR MAILBOX CAP
PRE-MANUF. MAILBOX

1"X1 1/2" TOP SIDE
SUPPORT BEYOND

1"X1 1/2" FRONT
SUPPORT BEYOND

2X10 BASE PANEL

9 3/4"

2X10 REAR PANEL

1 5/16"X1 5/16" CORNER
MOULDING; WM 204

1'-8"

DETAIL B-B

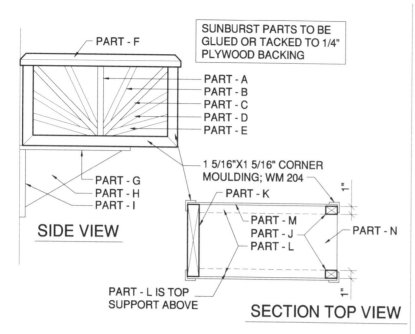

PART - F

SUNBURST PARTS TO BE
GLUED OR TACKED TO 1/4"
PLYWOOD BACKING

PART - A
PART - B
PART - C
PART - D
PART - E

1 5/16"X1 5/16" CORNER
MOULDING; WM 204

SIDE VIEW

PART - G
PART - H
PART - I

PART - K

PART - M
PART - J
PART - L

PART - N

1"

1"

PART - L IS TOP
SUPPORT ABOVE

SECTION TOP VIEW

PART CALLOUTS

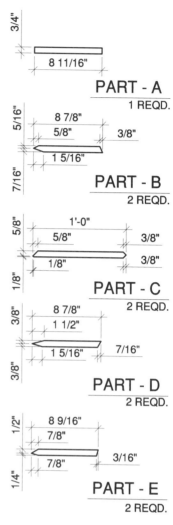

3/4"

8 11/16"

PART - A
1 REQD.

8 7/8"
5/8" 3/8"
1 5/16"
5/16"
7/16"

PART - B
2 REQD.

1'-0"
5/8" 3/8"
1/8" 3/8"
5/8"
1/8"

PART - C
2 REQD.

8 7/8"
1 1/2"
1 5/16" 7/16"
3/8"
3/8"

PART - D
2 REQD.

8 9/16"
7/8"
7/8" 3/16"
1/2"
1/4"

PART - E
2 REQD.

SUNBURST CUTTING

ALL PARTS CUT FROM
1/4"X3/4" CEDAR SCREEN
MOULDING; WM 142

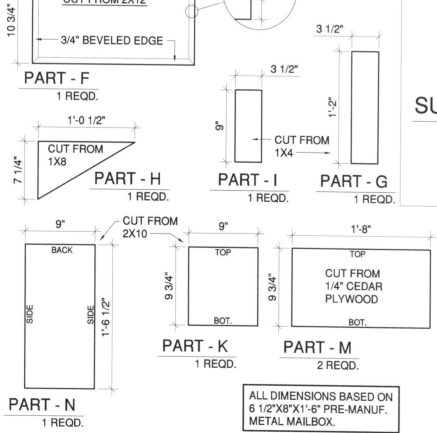

1'-9"

CUT FROM 2X12

3/4" BEVELED EDGE

10 3/4"

3/4"

PART - F
1 REQD.

1'-0 1/2"

CUT FROM
1X8

7 1/4"

PART - H
1 REQD.

3 1/2"

9"

CUT FROM
1X4

PART - I
1 REQD.

3 1/2"

1'-2"

PART - G
1 REQD.

9"

CUT FROM
2X10

BACK

SIDE

SIDE

1'-6 1/2"

PART - N
1 REQD.

9"

TOP

BOT.

9 3/4"

PART - K
1 REQD.

1'-8"

TOP

CUT FROM
1/4" CEDAR
PLYWOOD

BOT.

9 3/4"

PART - M
2 REQD.

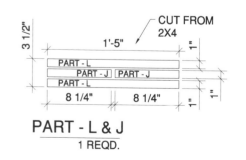

3 1/2"

CUT FROM
2X4

1'-5"

PART - L
PART - J   PART - J
PART - L

8 1/4"   8 1/4"

1"

1"

1"

PART - L & J
1 REQD.

ALL DIMENSIONS BASED ON
6 1/2"X8"X1'-6" PRE-MANUF.
METAL MAILBOX.

MAILBOX POST & BRACE

Item	Location	Qty	UM
60# Concrete Mix	Post	1	BG
4x4 - 8' Cedar	Post	1	EA
3" Dia. Newel Ball w/Screw	Post	1	EA
1x4 - 4' Cedar	Brace	1	EA
1x8 - 4' Cedar	Brace	1	EA
5# 6d Finish Box Nails	General Framing	1	EA
1# 4d Casing Nails	General Framing	1	EA
1# 2" Gold Screw	General Framing	1	EA

MAILBOX

Item	Location	Qty	UM
2x4 - 4' Cedar	Part L, J	1	EA
2x10 - 4' Cedar	Part K, N	1	EA
2x12 - 4' Cedar	Part F	1	EA
1/4" - 2'x4' Cedar Ply.	Part M	1	EA
1/4"x3/4" Cdr. Scrn. Mldg. (WM 142)	Part A, B, C, D, E	20	LF
1-5/16"x1-5/16" Cdr. Crnr. Mldg. (WM 204)	Edging	14	LF
Construction Adhesive	General	1	TB
Standard T1 Size Mailbox	Box	1	EA

THE KNOLLVIEW

HPM-1307

Need extra space for potting plants and storing garden tools? The gardener in your family will truly enjoy having his own space in this attractive gardening shed. Three operable windows and fixed clerestory windows above let in plenty of light. A built-in bench and three shelves keep your storage items organized and off the floor.

Dimensions for this potting shed are 8' X 8'.

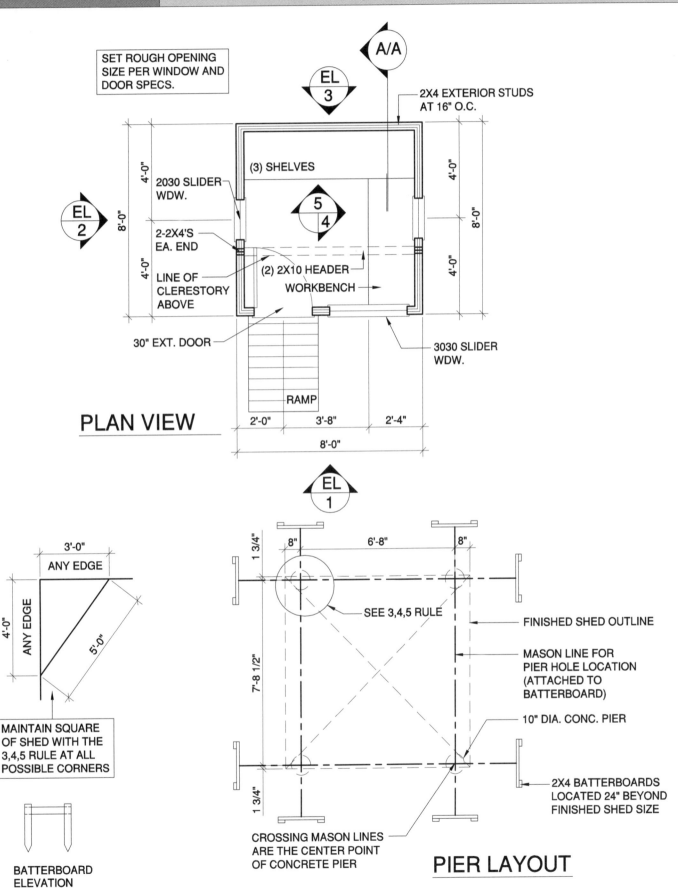

PLAN VIEW

SET ROUGH OPENING SIZE PER WINDOW AND DOOR SPECS.

2X4 EXTERIOR STUDS AT 16" O.C.

(3) SHELVES

2030 SLIDER WDW.

2-2X4'S EA. END

LINE OF CLERESTORY ABOVE

(2) 2X10 HEADER

WORKBENCH

30" EXT. DOOR

3030 SLIDER WDW.

RAMP

BATTERBOARD ELEVATION (TEMPORARY)

ANY EDGE

ANY EDGE

MAINTAIN SQUARE OF SHED WITH THE 3,4,5 RULE AT ALL POSSIBLE CORNERS

SEE 3,4,5 RULE

FINISHED SHED OUTLINE

MASON LINE FOR PIER HOLE LOCATION (ATTACHED TO BATTERBOARD)

10" DIA. CONC. PIER

2X4 BATTERBOARDS LOCATED 24" BEYOND FINISHED SHED SIZE

CROSSING MASON LINES ARE THE CENTER POINT OF CONCRETE PIER

PIER LAYOUT

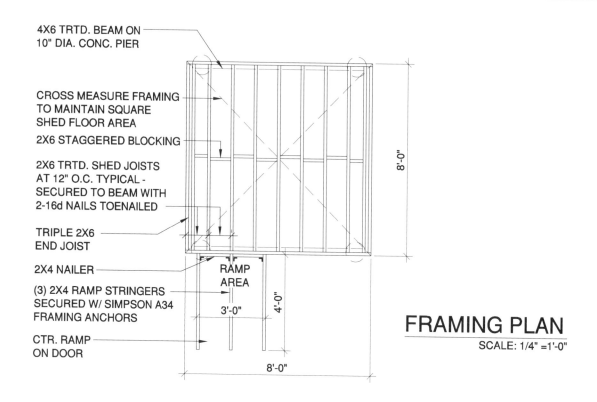

4X6 TRTD. BEAM ON
10" DIA. CONC. PIER

CROSS MEASURE FRAMING
TO MAINTAIN SQUARE
SHED FLOOR AREA

2X6 STAGGERED BLOCKING

2X6 TRTD. SHED JOISTS
AT 12" O.C. TYPICAL -
SECURED TO BEAM WITH
2-16d NAILS TOENAILED

TRIPLE 2X6
END JOIST

2X4 NAILER

(3) 2X4 RAMP STRINGERS
SECURED W/ SIMPSON A34
FRAMING ANCHORS

CTR. RAMP
ON DOOR

RAMP
AREA

8'-0"

3'-0"   4'-0"

8'-0"

FRAMING PLAN
SCALE: 1/4" =1'-0"

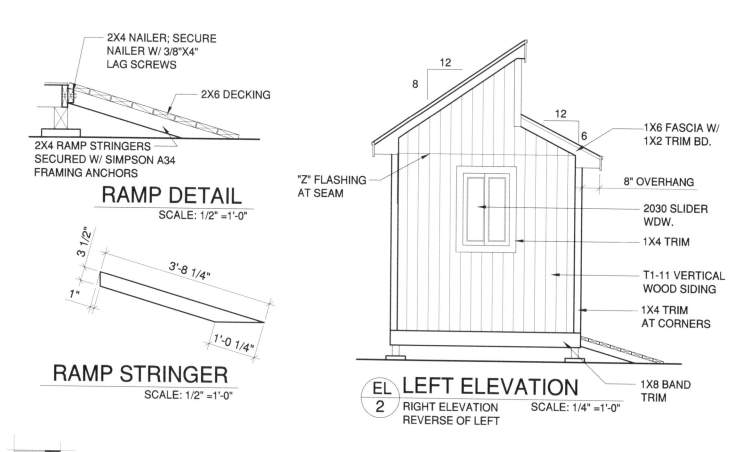

2X4 NAILER; SECURE
NAILER W/ 3/8"X4"
LAG SCREWS

2X6 DECKING

2X4 RAMP STRINGERS
SECURED W/ SIMPSON A34
FRAMING ANCHORS

RAMP DETAIL
SCALE: 1/2" =1'-0"

3 1/2"

3'-8 1/4"

1"

1'-0 1/4"

RAMP STRINGER
SCALE: 1/2" =1'-0"

12
8

12
6

1X6 FASCIA W/
1X2 TRIM BD.

8" OVERHANG

"Z" FLASHING
AT SEAM

2030 SLIDER
WDW.

1X4 TRIM

T1-11 VERTICAL
WOOD SIDING

1X4 TRIM
AT CORNERS

1X8 BAND
TRIM

EL
2

LEFT ELEVATION
RIGHT ELEVATION
REVERSE OF LEFT

SCALE: 1/4" =1'-0"

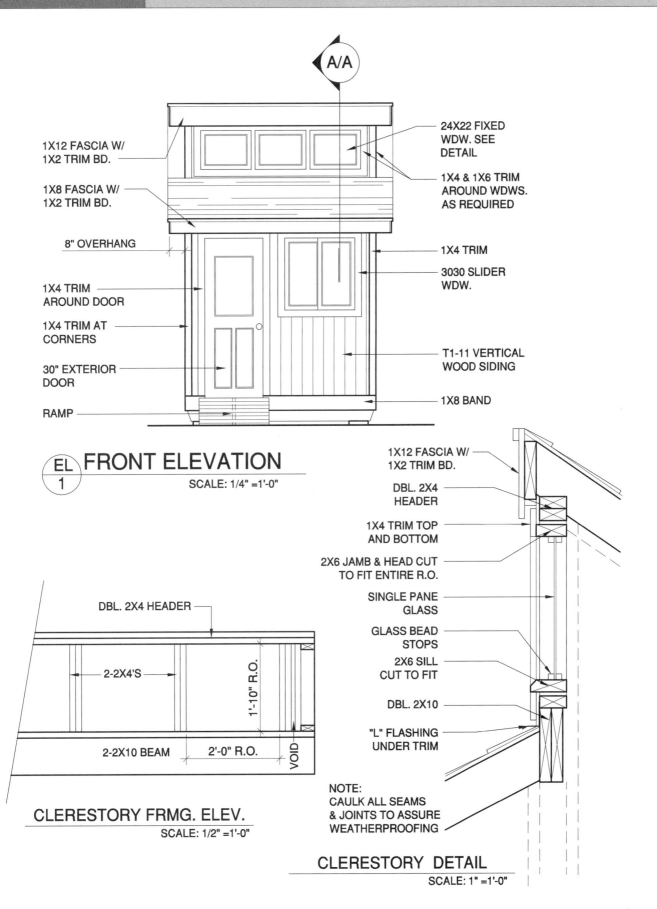

A/A

1X12 FASCIA W/
1X2 TRIM BD.

1X8 FASCIA W/
1X2 TRIM BD.

8" OVERHANG

1X4 TRIM
AROUND DOOR

1X4 TRIM AT
CORNERS

30" EXTERIOR
DOOR

RAMP

24X22 FIXED
WDW. SEE
DETAIL

1X4 & 1X6 TRIM
AROUND WDWS.
AS REQUIRED

1X4 TRIM

3030 SLIDER
WDW.

T1-11 VERTICAL
WOOD SIDING

1X8 BAND

EL 1 FRONT ELEVATION
SCALE: 1/4" =1'-0"

CLERESTORY FRMG. ELEV.
SCALE: 1/2" =1'-0"

DBL. 2X4 HEADER

2-2X4'S

1'-10" R.O.

2-2X10 BEAM   2'-0" R.O.

VOID

1X12 FASCIA W/
1X2 TRIM BD.

DBL. 2X4
HEADER

1X4 TRIM TOP
AND BOTTOM

2X6 JAMB & HEAD CUT
TO FIT ENTIRE R.O.

SINGLE PANE
GLASS

GLASS BEAD
STOPS

2X6 SILL
CUT TO FIT

DBL. 2X10

"L" FLASHING
UNDER TRIM

NOTE:
CAULK ALL SEAMS
& JOINTS TO ASSURE
WEATHERPROOFING

CLERESTORY DETAIL
SCALE: 1" =1'-0"

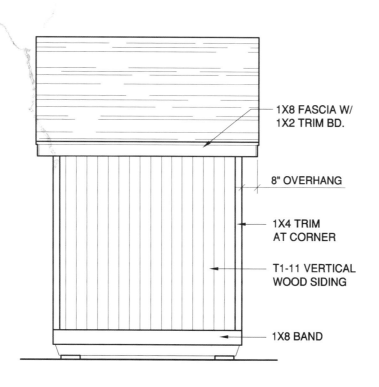

1X8 FASCIA W/
1X2 TRIM BD.

8" OVERHANG

1X4 TRIM
AT CORNER

T1-11 VERTICAL
WOOD SIDING

1X8 BAND

EL 3 REAR ELEVATION
SCALE: 1/4" =1'-0"

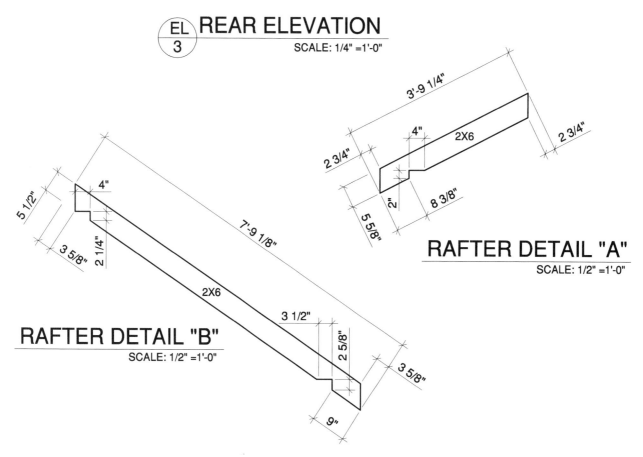

3'-9 1/4"

2 3/4"

4" 2X6

2 3/4"

2" 8 3/8"

5 5/8"

RAFTER DETAIL "A"
SCALE: 1/2" =1'-0"

5 1/2"

4"

3 5/8" 2 1/4"

7'-9 1/8"

2X6

3 1/2"

2 5/8"

RAFTER DETAIL "B"
SCALE: 1/2" =1'-0"

3 5/8"

9"

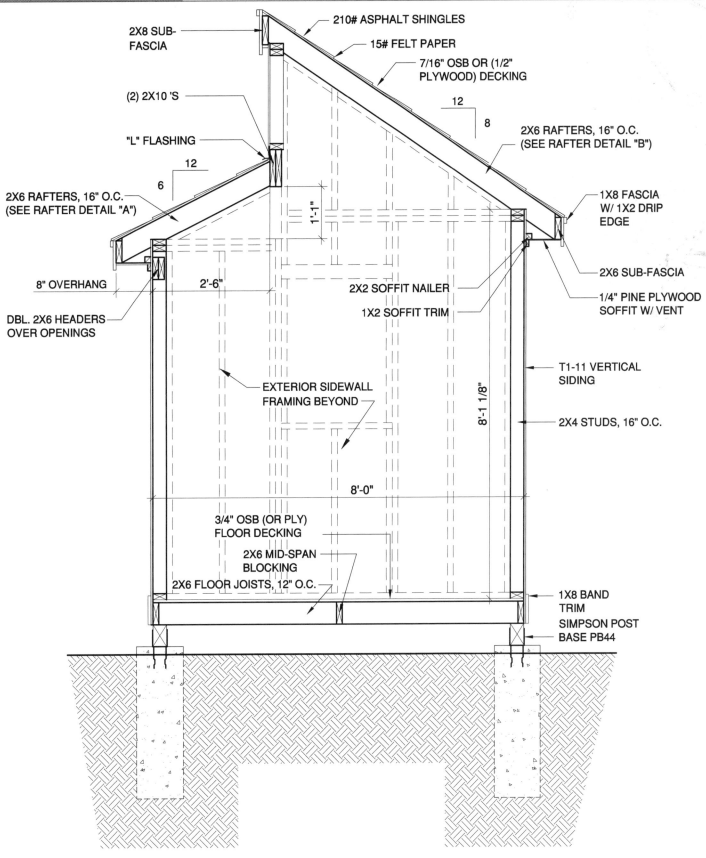

2X8 SUB-FASCIA

210# ASPHALT SHINGLES

15# FELT PAPER

7/16" OSB OR (1/2" PLYWOOD) DECKING

(2) 2X10 'S

12 / 8

"L" FLASHING

2X6 RAFTERS, 16" O.C. (SEE RAFTER DETAIL "B")

12 / 6

2X6 RAFTERS, 16" O.C. (SEE RAFTER DETAIL "A")

1X8 FASCIA W/ 1X2 DRIP EDGE

1'-1"

2X6 SUB-FASCIA

8" OVERHANG

2'-6"

2X2 SOFFIT NAILER

1X2 SOFFIT TRIM

1/4" PINE PLYWOOD SOFFIT W/ VENT

DBL. 2X6 HEADERS OVER OPENINGS

EXTERIOR SIDEWALL FRAMING BEYOND

T1-11 VERTICAL SIDING

8'-1 1/8"

2X4 STUDS, 16" O.C.

8'-0"

3/4" OSB (OR PLY) FLOOR DECKING

2X6 MID-SPAN BLOCKING

2X6 FLOOR JOISTS, 12" O.C.

1X8 BAND TRIM

SIMPSON POST BASE PB44

CROSS SECTION

A-A

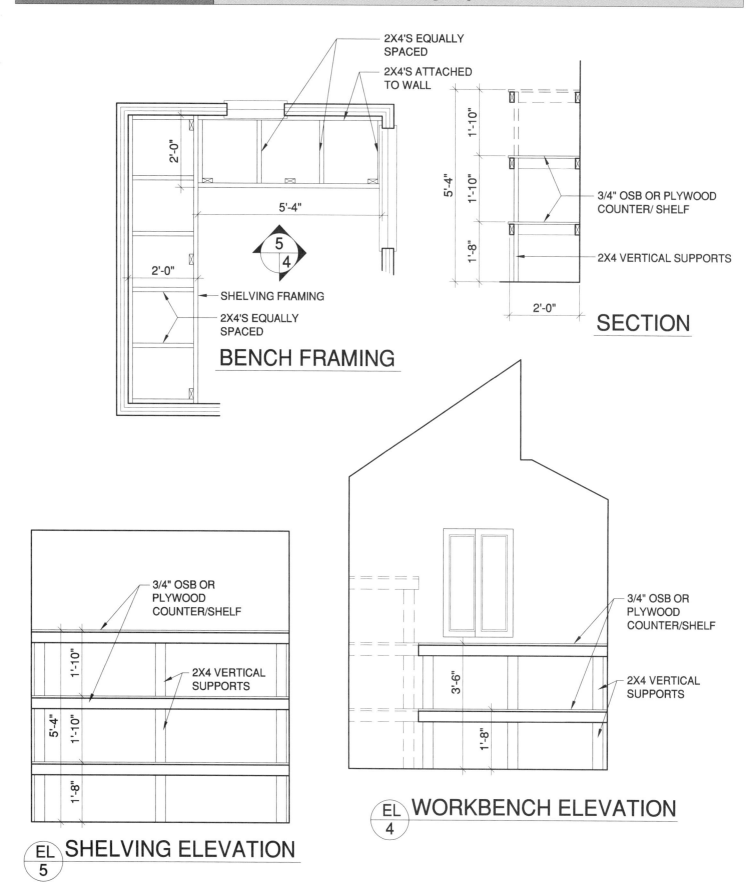

2X4'S EQUALLY SPACED

2X4'S ATTACHED TO WALL

2'-0"

5'-4"

5 / 4

2'-0"

SHELVING FRAMING

2X4'S EQUALLY SPACED

BENCH FRAMING

1'-10"

1'-10"

5'-4"

1'-8"

3/4" OSB OR PLYWOOD COUNTER/ SHELF

2X4 VERTICAL SUPPORTS

2'-0"

SECTION

3/4" OSB OR PLYWOOD COUNTER/SHELF

2X4 VERTICAL SUPPORTS

1'-10"

5'-4"

1'-10"

1'-8"

EL / 5 ## SHELVING ELEVATION

3/4" OSB OR PLYWOOD COUNTER/SHELF

2X4 VERTICAL SUPPORTS

3'-6"

1'-8"

EL / 4 ## WORKBENCH ELEVATION

FOUNDATION

Item	Location	Qty	UM
60# Concrete Mix	Pier	20	BG
10"x48" Fiber Tube	Pier	4	EA
2x4 - 10' Std. & Btr.	Batterboard	5	EA
Post Base (PB44)	Pier	4	EA
1/2" Hex. Hd. Nut	Post Base	8	EA
1/2" x4-1/2" Bolt	Post Base	8	EA
1/2" Washer	Post Base	16	EA
Crushed Gravel	Pier	8	BG

FLOOR

Item	Location	Qty	UM
4x6 - 8' Treated	Beam	2	EA
2x6 - 8' Treated	Floor Joist/Blocking	17	EA
3/4" OSB (Ply.)	Floor Decking	2	EA
Framing Anchor (A34)	Floor Framing	8	EA
2x4 - 8' Treated	Nailer/Stringer	2	EA
2x6 - 12' Treated	Decking	2	EA
3/8"x4" Lag Screws	Ramp Nailer	4	EA
3/8"x1-1/2" Washer	Ramp Nailer	4	EA
5# 16d Galv. Nails	General Framing	1	EA
5# 8d Ctd. Box Nails	General Framing	1	EA
1# 2-1/2" Ctd. Ext. Screws	General Framing	1	EA
Construction Adhesive	Floor Decking	2	TB

WALL FRAMING

Item	Location	Qty	UM
2x4 - 8' Treated	Bottom Plate	4	EA
2x4 - 96" Stud Grade	Wall/Gable/Clerestory	40	EA
2x4 - 96" Stud Grade	Crpl./Sill/Blkg./Plate	14	EA
2x4 - 8' Std. & Btr.	Top/Cap Plate	8	EA
2x4 - 8' Std. & Btr.	Clerestory Plate	3	EA
2x6 - 10' Std. & Btr.	Header	2	EA
2x10 - 8' Std. & Btr.	Header	2	EA
3/8" T1-11 Siding	Wall Sheathing/Siding	10	EA
5# 6d Galv. Nails	General Framing	2	EA
5# 8d Ctd. Box Nails	General Framing	2	EA
1x6 - 10' Std. & Btr.	Bracing	4	EA

CEILING/ROOF

Item	Location	Qty	UM
2x6 - 8' Std. & Btr.	Rafter	12	EA
2x6 - 10' Std. & Btr.	Sub-Fascia	2	EA
2x8 - 10' Std. & Btr.	Sub-Fascia	1	EA
2x4 - 8' Std. & Btr.	Ladder Rake/Blocking	7	EA
2x2 - 8' #2 & Btr. S4S	Soffit Nailer	2	EA
1x4 - 10' #2 & Btr. (Rip-1x2)	Soffit Trim	1	EA
1x6 - 12' #2 & Btr. S4S	Fascia	2	EA
1x8 - 10' #2 & Btr. S4S	Fascia	2	EA
1x12 - 10' #2 & Btr. S4S	Fascia	1	EA
7/16" OSB (Ply.)	Roof Decking	4	EA
3 - Tab Shingle 20 Yr.	Shingle	4	BN
15-lb. Asphalt Rfg. Felt	Roofing	1	RL
"L" Flashing - 10' Roof - Wall	Clerestory	1	EA
5# 8d Ctd. Box Nails	General Framing	2	EA
5# 10d Bright Box Nails	General Framing	2	EA
5# 16d Galv. Nails	General Framing	1	EA
5# 1/2" Roofing Nails	Roofing Felt	1	EA
5# 1-1/4" Roofing Nails	Shingle	2	EA
5# 6d Galv. Box Nails	General Framing	1	EA
5# 6d Galv. Finish Nails	Siding/Soffit	1	EA

EXTERIOR TRIM & ACCESSORIES

Item	Location	Qty	UM
1x2 - 8' Std. & Btr. (Rip-1x1)	Window Stop	3	EA
1x4 - 10' #2 & Btr. (Rip-1x2)	Fascia/Eave	3	EA
1x4 - 10' #2 & Btr.	Corner/Dr./Wdw. Trim	9	EA
1x6 - 8' #2 & Btr.	Window Trim	1	EA
1x 8 - 10' #2 & Btr.	Band Trim	4	EA
1/4" Plywood (Sanded)	Soffit Material	2	EA
2x6 - 8' Std. & Btr.	Window Jamb	3	EA
2x4 - 8' Std. & Btr.	Shelf Frame	22	EA
3/4" OSB (Ply.)	Shelf	3	EA
14"x6" Metal Soffit Vent	Soffit	4	EA
Single Pane Glass (20"x18")	Window	3	EA
30"x80" Exterior Door	Exterior Door	1	EA
2030 Slider Window	Window	2	EA
3030 Slider Window	Window	1	EA
Lockset/Deadbolt	Exterior Door	1	EA
5# 6d Galv. Finish Nails	Siding/Soffit	4	EA
5# 8d Galv. Finish Nails	Window/Door	1	EA
10 oz. - Paintable Caulk	Siding/Trim	6	TB
3/8" - 10' "Z" - Bar Flashing	Horz. Siding Seam	2	EA
4" - 10' "Z" Flashing	Window/Door	2	EA

THE VILLA

HPM-1714

Fill up this wonderful flower box with colorful annuals or simple greenery to create a beautiful outdoor ambience on your deck or patio. Place a box in each corner or arrange them in a row for a more dramatic effect. Sunburst detailing adds interest and visually connects each backyard accessory that you construct.

Dimensions for this flower box are 2' X 2'.

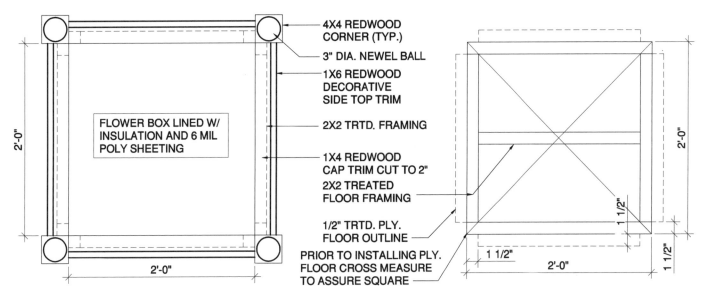

4X4 REDWOOD CORNER (TYP.)

3" DIA. NEWEL BALL

1X6 REDWOOD DECORATIVE SIDE TOP TRIM

2X2 TRTD. FRAMING

1X4 REDWOOD CAP TRIM CUT TO 2"

2X2 TREATED FLOOR FRAMING

1/2" TRTD. PLY. FLOOR OUTLINE

PRIOR TO INSTALLING PLY. FLOOR CROSS MEASURE TO ASSURE SQUARE

FLOWER BOX LINED W/ INSULATION AND 6 MIL POLY SHEETING

2'-0"

2'-0"

TOP VIEW

2'-0"

1 1/2"

1 1/2"

2'-0"

1 1/2"

FLOOR FRAMING

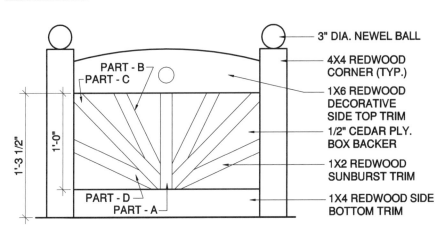

3" DIA. NEWEL BALL

4X4 REDWOOD CORNER (TYP.)

1X6 REDWOOD DECORATIVE SIDE TOP TRIM

1/2" CEDAR PLY. BOX BACKER

1X2 REDWOOD SUNBURST TRIM

1X4 REDWOOD SIDE BOTTOM TRIM

PART - B
PART - C

PART - D
PART - A

1'-0"

1'-3 1/2"

ELEVATION

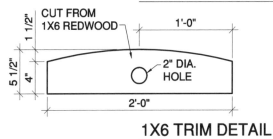

CUT FROM 1X6 REDWOOD

2" DIA. HOLE

1'-0"

1 1/2"

5 1/2"

4"

2'-0"

1X6 TRIM DETAIL

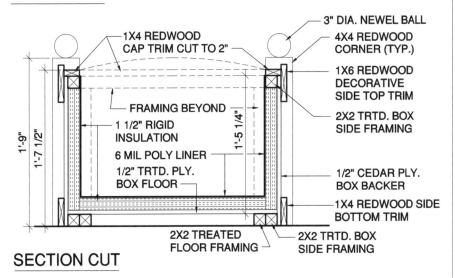

1X4 REDWOOD CAP TRIM CUT TO 2"

FRAMING BEYOND

1 1/2" RIGID INSULATION

6 MIL POLY LINER

1/2" TRTD. PLY. BOX FLOOR

2X2 TREATED FLOOR FRAMING

3" DIA. NEWEL BALL

4X4 REDWOOD CORNER (TYP.)

1X6 REDWOOD DECORATIVE SIDE TOP TRIM

2X2 TRTD. BOX SIDE FRAMING

1/2" CEDAR PLY. BOX BACKER

1X4 REDWOOD SIDE BOTTOM TRIM

2X2 TRTD. BOX SIDE FRAMING

1'-9"

1'-7 1/2"

1'-5 1/4"

SECTION CUT

SUNBURST CUTTING

1'-0"

1 1/2"

PART - A
1 REQD.

11 13/16"

1 1/4"

3/4"

2 11/16"

5/8"

7/8"

PART - B
2 REQD.

1'-4 7/16"

1 1/4"

3/4"

3/4"

1/4"

3/4"

1 1/4"

3/4"

PART - C
2 REQD.

1'-0 9/16"

3 3/16"

5/8"

11/16"

1 3/16"

5/16"

PART - D
2 REQD.

FLOWER BOX FLOOR MATERIAL

Item	Location	Qty	UM
2x2 - 6' Treated	Base	3	EA
1/2" Treated Plywood	Base	1	EA
5# 16d Galv. Nails	General Framing	1	EA
5# 8d Galv. Nails	General Framing	1	EA

FLOWER BOX FRAME MATERIAL

Item	Location	Qty	UM
4x4 - 8' Redwood	Corner Post	1	EA
3" Dia. Newel Ball w/Screw	Corner Post	4	EA
2x2 - 8' Treated	Top/Side Frame	3	EA
1/2" Cedar Plywood	Box Backer	1	EA
1-1/2" Rigid Insulation	Box Liner	1	EA
6-Mil Poly Sheeting	Box Liner	1	RI
5# 16d Galv. Nails	General Framing	1	EA
5# 8d Galv. Nails	General Framing	1	EA
5# 8d Coated Box Nails	Finish Framing	1	EA

FLOWER BOX TRIM MATERIAL

Item	Location	Qty	UM
1x2 - 8' Redwood	Sunburst Trim	4	EA
1x4 - 8' Redwood	Bottom Trim	1	EA
1x4 - 8' Redwood (Cut to 2")	Cap	1	EA
1x6 - 8' Redwood	Top/Decorative Trim	2	EA
5# 8d Coated Box Nails	Finish Framing	1	EA
Construction Adhesive	Trim	1	EA

THE BOUNTIFUL

HPM-1712

Dress up your home's exterior with this decorative window box. Designed for a 3-ft.-wide window, the box can be customized to fit the size and location of the windows on your home, or to accommodate the plants or flowers you desire.

Dimensions for this window box are 3' X 1'4".

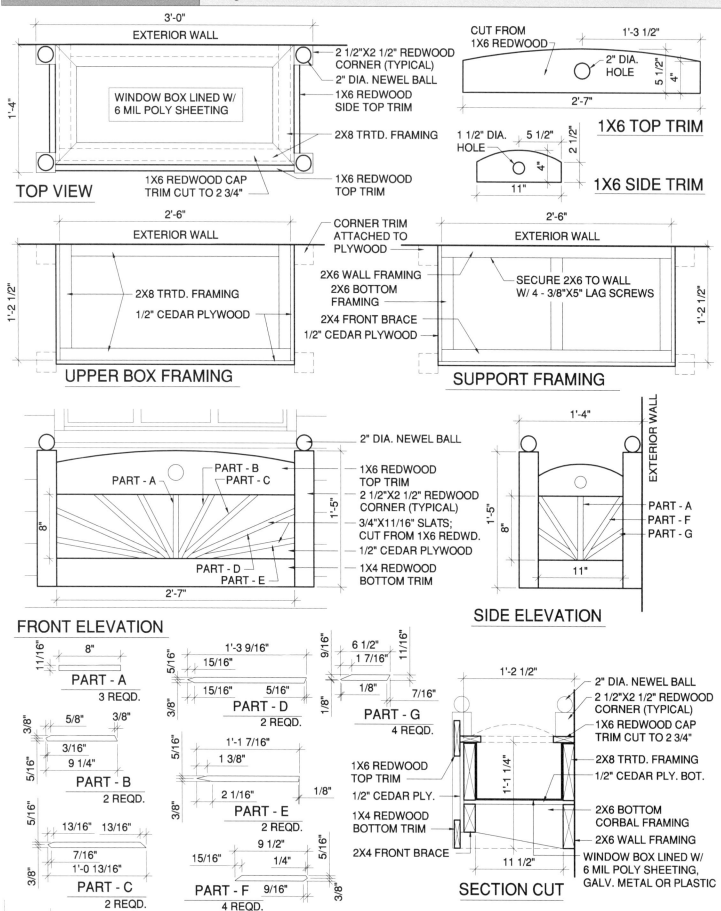

TOP VIEW

3'-0"
EXTERIOR WALL
1'-4"
WINDOW BOX LINED W/ 6 MIL POLY SHEETING

2 1/2"X2 1/2" REDWOOD CORNER (TYPICAL)
2" DIA. NEWEL BALL
1X6 REDWOOD SIDE TOP TRIM
2X8 TRTD. FRAMING
1X6 REDWOOD CAP TRIM CUT TO 2 3/4"
1X6 REDWOOD TOP TRIM

CUT FROM 1X6 REDWOOD
1'-3 1/2"
2" DIA. HOLE
5 1/2"
4"
2'-7"
1X6 TOP TRIM

1 1/2" DIA. HOLE
5 1/2"
2 1/2"
4"
11"
1X6 SIDE TRIM

UPPER BOX FRAMING

2'-6"
EXTERIOR WALL
1'-2 1/2"
2X8 TRTD. FRAMING
1/2" CEDAR PLYWOOD

CORNER TRIM ATTACHED TO PLYWOOD
2X6 WALL FRAMING
2X6 BOTTOM FRAMING
2X4 FRONT BRACE
1/2" CEDAR PLYWOOD

SUPPORT FRAMING

2'-6"
EXTERIOR WALL
SECURE 2X6 TO WALL W/ 4 - 3/8"X5" LAG SCREWS
1'-2 1/2"

FRONT ELEVATION

8"
1'-5"
2'-7"
PART - A
PART - B
PART - C
PART - D
PART - E

2" DIA. NEWEL BALL
1X6 REDWOOD TOP TRIM
2 1/2"X2 1/2" REDWOOD CORNER (TYPICAL)
3/4"X11/16" SLATS; CUT FROM 1X6 REDWD.
1/2" CEDAR PLYWOOD
1X4 REDWOOD BOTTOM TRIM

SIDE ELEVATION

1'-4"
EXTERIOR WALL
8"
1'-5"
11"
PART - A
PART - F
PART - G

PART - A
11/16"
8"
3 REQD.

PART - B
3/8"
5/8"
3/8"
3/16"
9 1/4"
5/16"
2 REQD.

PART - C
5/16"
13/16"
13/16"
7/16"
1'-0 13/16"
3/8"
2 REQD.

PART - D
5/16"
1'-3 9/16"
15/16"
15/16"
5/16"
3/8"
2 REQD.

PART - E
5/16"
1'-1 7/16"
1 3/8"
2 1/16"
1/8"
3/8"
2 REQD.

PART - F
15/16"
9 1/2"
1/4"
9/16"
5/16"
3/8"
4 REQD.

PART - G
9/16"
6 1/2"
1 7/16"
11/16"
1/8"
7/16"
4 REQD.

SECTION CUT

1'-2 1/2"
1'-1 1/4"
11 1/2"
1X6 REDWOOD TOP TRIM
1/2" CEDAR PLY.
1X4 REDWOOD BOTTOM TRIM
2X4 FRONT BRACE

2" DIA. NEWEL BALL
2 1/2"X2 1/2" REDWOOD CORNER (TYPICAL)
1X6 REDWOOD CAP TRIM CUT TO 2 3/4"
2X8 TRTD. FRAMING
1/2" CEDAR PLY. BOT.
2X6 BOTTOM CORBAL FRAMING
2X6 WALL FRAMING
WINDOW BOX LINED W/ 6 MIL POLY SHEETING, GALV. METAL OR PLASTIC

FLOWER BOX SUPPORT MATERIAL

Item	Location	Qty	UM
2x6 - 8' Treated	Wall/Corbal Framing	1	EA
2x4 - 8' Treated	Front Brace	1	EA
3/8"x5" Lag Screws	Wall Frame	4	EA
3/8" Washer	Lag Screw	4	EA

FLOWER BOX FRAME MATERIAL

Item	Location	Qty	UM
2x8 - 8' Treated	Upper Frame	1	EA
1/2" - 4x4 Cedar Plywood	Box Backer/Base	1	EA
6-Mil Poly Sheeting	Box Liner	1	RI

FLOWER BOX TRIM MATERIAL

Item	Location	Qty	UM
4x4 - 6' Redwood	2-1/2"x2-1/2" Corner	1	EA
2" Dia. Newel Ball w/Screw	Corner Post	4	EA
1x4 - 8' Redwood	Bottom Trim	1	EA
1x6 - 8' Redwood	Top/Side/Cap/Sunburst	3	EA
1# 2" Gold Screw	General Framing	3	EA
1# 2-1/2" Gold Screw	General Framing	3	EA
1# 6d Coated Box Nails	Finish Framing	1	EA
1# 4d Coated Finish Nails	Finish Framing	2	EA
Construction Adhesive	Trim	1	TB

THE BRIARGATE

HPM-1708

Create a charming welcome to your yard or a lovely complement to your garden with this smart arbor. The handsome rails and keystones give it a traditional look, which can be embellished with vines or colorful blossoms. Rafters across the top can support hanging plants or offer you some relief from the sun on a hot day.

Dimensions for this arbor are 4'6" X 4'6".

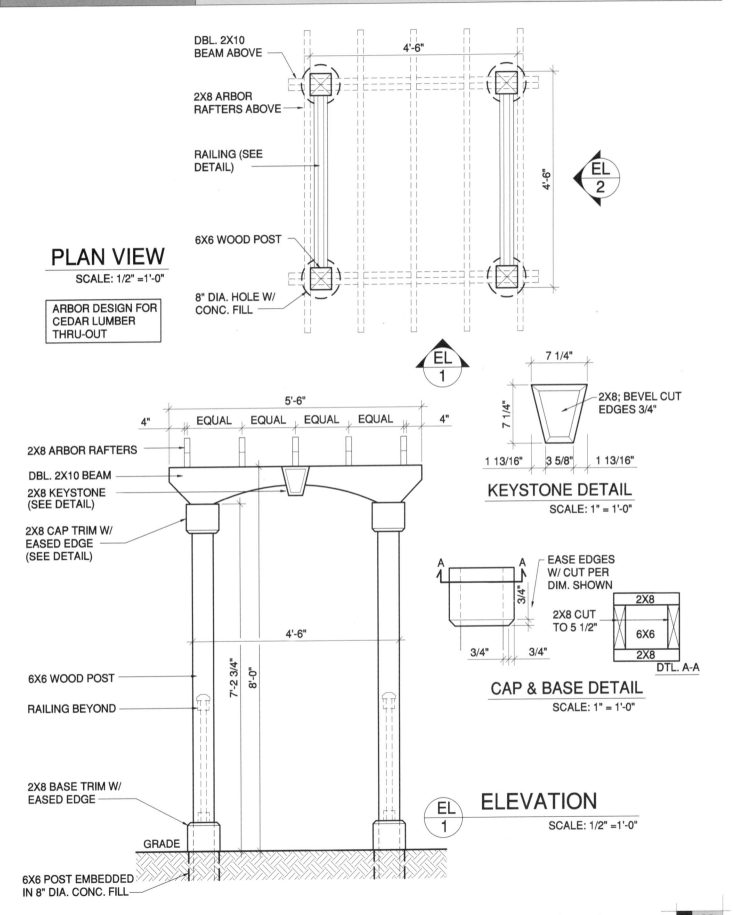

DBL. 2X10 BEAM ABOVE

2X8 ARBOR RAFTERS ABOVE

RAILING (SEE DETAIL)

4'-6"

4'-6"

EL 2

6X6 WOOD POST

PLAN VIEW
SCALE: 1/2" =1'-0"

ARBOR DESIGN FOR CEDAR LUMBER THRU-OUT

8" DIA. HOLE W/ CONC. FILL

EL 1

7 1/4"

7 1/4"

2X8; BEVEL CUT EDGES 3/4"

1 13/16" 3 5/8" 1 13/16"

KEYSTONE DETAIL
SCALE: 1" = 1'-0"

5'-6"

4" EQUAL EQUAL EQUAL EQUAL 4"

2X8 ARBOR RAFTERS

DBL. 2X10 BEAM

2X8 KEYSTONE (SEE DETAIL)

2X8 CAP TRIM W/ EASED EDGE (SEE DETAIL)

A A EASE EDGES W/ CUT PER DIM. SHOWN

3/4"

2X8 CUT TO 5 1/2"

2X8

6X6

2X8

3/4" 3/4"

3/4" 3/4"

DTL. A-A

CAP & BASE DETAIL
SCALE: 1" = 1'-0"

4'-6"

7'-2 3/4"

8'-0"

6X6 WOOD POST

RAILING BEYOND

2X8 BASE TRIM W/ EASED EDGE

EL 1

ELEVATION
SCALE: 1/2" =1'-0"

GRADE

6X6 POST EMBEDDED IN 8" DIA. CONC. FILL

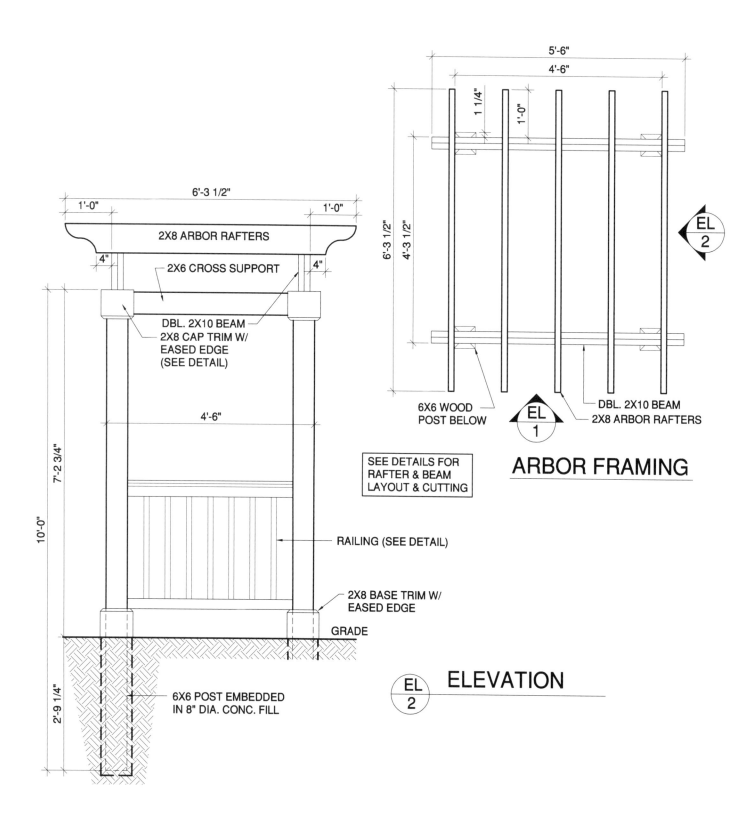

6'-3 1/2"

1'-0"

2X8 ARBOR RAFTERS

4"

2X6 CROSS SUPPORT

4"

DBL. 2X10 BEAM
2X8 CAP TRIM W/
EASED EDGE
(SEE DETAIL)

4'-6"

7'-2 3/4"

10'-0"

RAILING (SEE DETAIL)

2X8 BASE TRIM W/
EASED EDGE

GRADE

2'-9 1/4"

6X6 POST EMBEDDED
IN 8" DIA. CONC. FILL

5'-6"

4'-6"

1 1/4"

1'-0"

6'-3 1/2"

4'-3 1/2"

EL 2

6X6 WOOD
POST BELOW

EL 1

DBL. 2X10 BEAM
2X8 ARBOR RAFTERS

ARBOR FRAMING

SEE DETAILS FOR
RAFTER & BEAM
LAYOUT & CUTTING

EL 2 **ELEVATION**

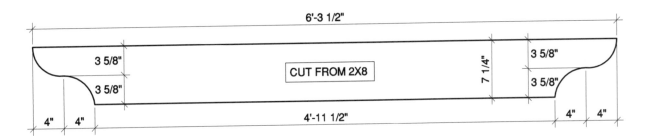

ARBOR RAFTER
SCALE: 1" =1'-0"

Dimensions: 6'-3 1/2", 3 5/8", 3 5/8", CUT FROM 2X8, 7 1/4", 3 5/8", 3 5/8", 4", 4", 4'-11 1/2", 4", 4"

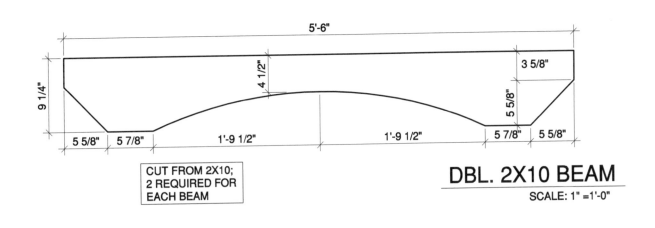

CUT FROM 2X10;
2 REQUIRED FOR
EACH BEAM

DBL. 2X10 BEAM
SCALE: 1" =1'-0"

Dimensions: 5'-6", 4 1/2", 3 5/8", 9 1/4", 5 5/8", 5 5/8", 5 7/8", 1'-9 1/2", 1'-9 1/2", 5 7/8", 5 5/8"

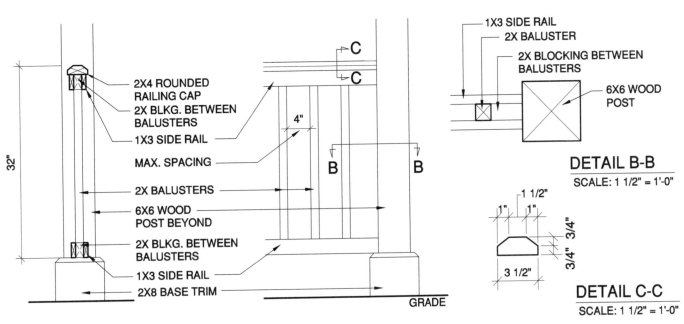

RAILING DETAILS
SCALE: 3/4" = 1'-0"

2X4 ROUNDED RAILING CAP
2X BLKG. BETWEEN BALUSTERS
1X3 SIDE RAIL
MAX. SPACING
2X BALUSTERS
6X6 WOOD POST BEYOND
2X BLKG. BETWEEN BALUSTERS
1X3 SIDE RAIL
2X8 BASE TRIM
32"
4"
GRADE
B B
C C

DETAIL B-B
SCALE: 1 1/2" = 1'-0"

1X3 SIDE RAIL
2X BALUSTER
2X BLOCKING BETWEEN BALUSTERS
6X6 WOOD POST

DETAIL C-C
SCALE: 1 1/2" = 1'-0"

1 1/2", 1", 1", 3/4", 3/4", 3 1/2"

ARBOR FRAMING

Item	Location	Qty	UM
60# Concrete Mix	Post	8	BG
6x6 - 10' Cedar	Post	4	EA
2x6 - 8' Cedar	Cross Support	1	EA
2x8 - 8' Cedar	Arbor Rafter	5	EA
2x10 - 6' Cedar	Beam	4	EA
5# 16d Galv. Nails	General Framing	3	EA
5# 8d Galv. Nails	General Framing	3	EA
1# 2" Coated Screws	General Framing	2	EA
1# 2-1/2" Coated Screws	General Framing	2	EA
5# 8d Coated Box Nails	General Framing	3	EA

TRIM/RAILING

Item	Location	Qty	UM
2x8 - 8' Cedar	Cap/Base/Keystone Trim	10	EA
2x4 - 8' Cedar	Cap Rail	1	EA
1x3 - 8' Cedar	Side Rail	4	EA
2x3 - 8' Cedar	Baluster Blocking	2	EA
2x2 - 3' Cedar	Baluster	16	EA

THE SPRINGHILL

HPM-1709

Read a book or simply enjoy the sights and sounds of nature in this stylish arbor/bench combination. Arbors are excellent structures for growing vines and displaying colorful plants. This one is made even more appealing with the addition of two comfortable benches. Discover the simpler times of days gone by as you sip lemonade, visit with the neighbors or take an afternoon nap.

Dimensions for this arbor/bench are 8' X 6'.

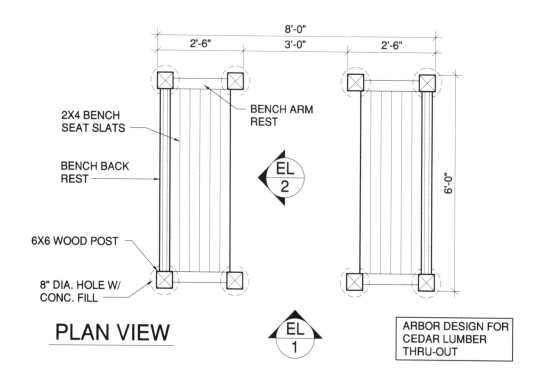

8'-0"

2'-6"   3'-0"   2'-6"

6'-0"

2X4 BENCH
SEAT SLATS

BENCH ARM
REST

BENCH BACK
REST

6X6 WOOD POST

8" DIA. HOLE W/
CONC. FILL

EL 2

EL 1

PLAN VIEW

ARBOR DESIGN FOR
CEDAR LUMBER
THRU-OUT

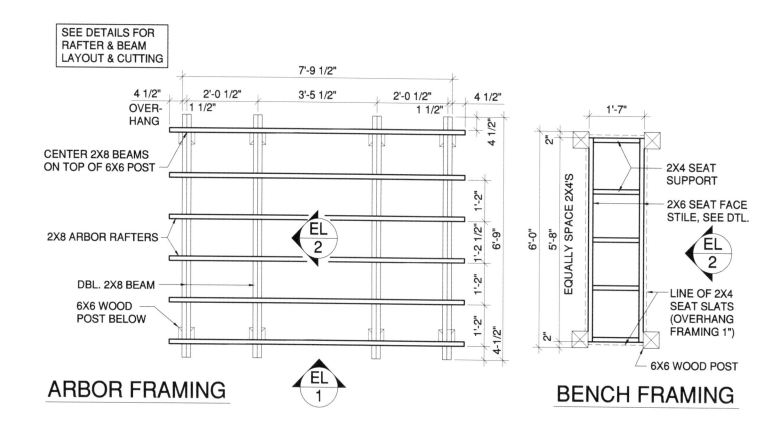

SEE DETAILS FOR
RAFTER & BEAM
LAYOUT & CUTTING

7'-9 1/2"

4 1/2"
OVER-
HANG

2'-0 1/2"   3'-5 1/2"   2'-0 1/2"   4 1/2"

1 1/2"   1 1/2"

4 1/2"

CENTER 2X8 BEAMS
ON TOP OF 6X6 POST

1'-2"
1'-2 1/2"
1'-2"   6'-9"
1'-2"
4-1/2"

2X8 ARBOR RAFTERS

DBL. 2X8 BEAM

6X6 WOOD
POST BELOW

EL 2

ARBOR FRAMING

EL 1

1'-7"

2"

6'-0"   5'-8"   EQUALLY SPACE 2X4'S

2"

2X4 SEAT
SUPPORT

2X6 SEAT FACE
STILE, SEE DTL.

EL 2

LINE OF 2X4
SEAT SLATS
(OVERHANG
FRAMING 1")

6X6 WOOD POST

BENCH FRAMING

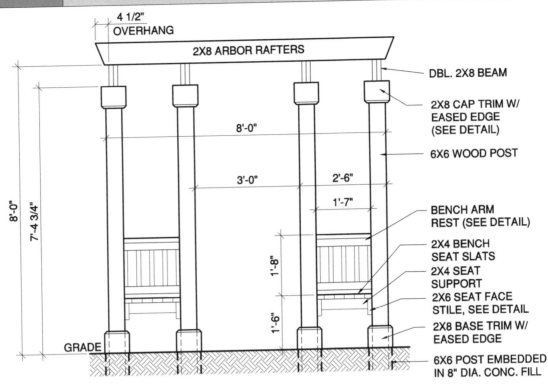

4 1/2"
OVERHANG

2X8 ARBOR RAFTERS

DBL. 2X8 BEAM

2X8 CAP TRIM W/
EASED EDGE
(SEE DETAIL)

6X6 WOOD POST

8'-0"

3'-0"

2'-6"

1'-7"

BENCH ARM
REST (SEE DETAIL)

2X4 BENCH
SEAT SLATS

2X4 SEAT
SUPPORT

2X6 SEAT FACE
STILE, SEE DETAIL

2X8 BASE TRIM W/
EASED EDGE

6X6 POST EMBEDDED
IN 8" DIA. CONC. FILL

8'-0"

7'-4 3/4"

1'-8"

1'-6"

GRADE

EL 1 **ELEVATION**
SCALE: 3/8" =1'-0"

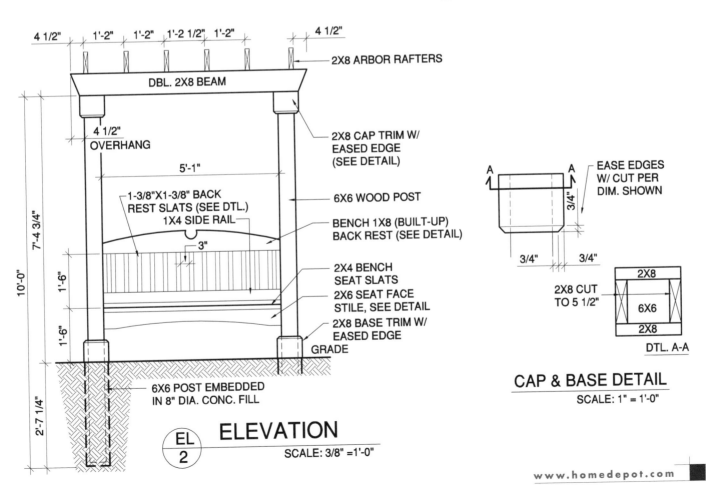

4 1/2"   1'-2"   1'-2"   1'-2 1/2"   1'-2"   4 1/2"

2X8 ARBOR RAFTERS

DBL. 2X8 BEAM

4 1/2"
OVERHANG

2X8 CAP TRIM W/
EASED EDGE
(SEE DETAIL)

5'-1"

6X6 WOOD POST

1-3/8"X1-3/8" BACK
REST SLATS (SEE DTL.)
1X4 SIDE RAIL

3"

BENCH 1X8 (BUILT-UP)
BACK REST (SEE DETAIL)

2X4 BENCH
SEAT SLATS

2X6 SEAT FACE
STILE, SEE DETAIL

2X8 BASE TRIM W/
EASED EDGE

GRADE

6X6 POST EMBEDDED
IN 8" DIA. CONC. FILL

10'-0"

7'-4 3/4"

1'-6"

1'-6"

2'-7 1/4"

EL 2 **ELEVATION**
SCALE: 3/8" =1'-0"

A — A

EASE EDGES
W/ CUT PER
DIM. SHOWN

3/4"

3/4"   3/4"

2X8 CUT
TO 5 1/2"

2X8	
	6X6
2X8	

DTL. A-A

CAP & BASE DETAIL
SCALE: 1" = 1'-0"

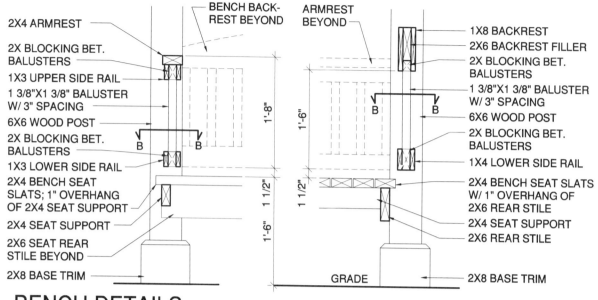

2X4 ARMREST

2X BLOCKING BET. BALUSTERS

1X3 UPPER SIDE RAIL

1 3/8"X1 3/8" BALUSTER W/ 3" SPACING

6X6 WOOD POST

2X BLOCKING BET. BALUSTERS

1X3 LOWER SIDE RAIL

2X4 BENCH SEAT SLATS; 1" OVERHANG OF 2X4 SEAT SUPPORT

2X4 SEAT SUPPORT

2X6 SEAT REAR STILE BEYOND

2X8 BASE TRIM

BENCH BACK-REST BEYOND

ARMREST BEYOND

1X8 BACKREST

2X6 BACKREST FILLER

2X BLOCKING BET. BALUSTERS

1 3/8"X1 3/8" BALUSTER W/ 3" SPACING

6X6 WOOD POST

2X BLOCKING BET. BALUSTERS

1X4 LOWER SIDE RAIL

2X4 BENCH SEAT SLATS W/ 1" OVERHANG OF 2X6 REAR STILE

2X4 SEAT SUPPORT

2X6 REAR STILE

GRADE

2X8 BASE TRIM

BENCH DETAILS

SCALE: 3/4" = 1'-0"

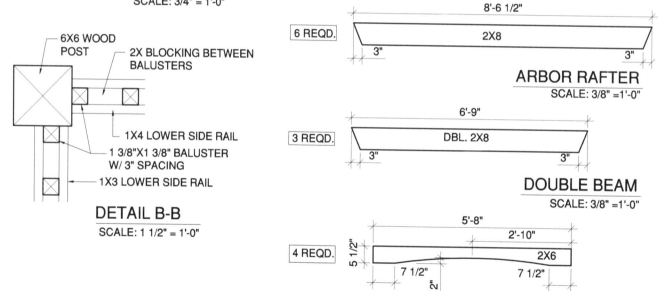

6X6 WOOD POST

2X BLOCKING BETWEEN BALUSTERS

1X4 LOWER SIDE RAIL

1 3/8"X1 3/8" BALUSTER W/ 3" SPACING

1X3 LOWER SIDE RAIL

DETAIL B-B

SCALE: 1 1/2" = 1'-0"

6 REQD. — 8'-6 1/2" — 2X8 — 3" — 3"

ARBOR RAFTER

SCALE: 3/8" =1'-0"

3 REQD. — 6'-9" — DBL. 2X8 — 3" — 3"

DOUBLE BEAM

SCALE: 3/8" =1'-0"

4 REQD. — 5'-8" — 2'-10" — 2X6 — 5 1/2" — 7 1/2" — 7 1/2" — 2"

FRONT/REAR SEAT STILE

SCALE: 3/8" =1'-0"

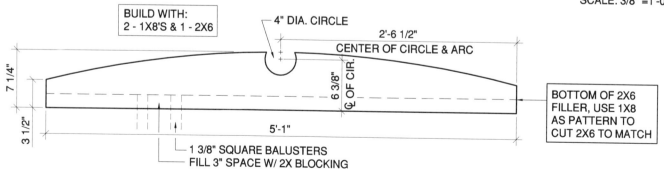

BUILD WITH: 2 - 1X8'S & 1 - 2X6

4" DIA. CIRCLE

2'-6 1/2"

CENTER OF CIRCLE & ARC

6 3/8"

℄ OF CIR.

7 1/4"

3 1/2"

5'-1"

1 3/8" SQUARE BALUSTERS

FILL 3" SPACE W/ 2X BLOCKING

BOTTOM OF 2X6 FILLER, USE 1X8 AS PATTERN TO CUT 2X6 TO MATCH

SEAT BACKREST

SCALE: 1" = 1'-0"

ARBOR FRAMING

Item	Location	Qty	UM
60# Concrete Mix	Post	16	BG
6x6 - 10' Cedar	Post	8	EA
2x8 - 8' Cedar	Beam	8	EA
2x8 - 10' Cedar	Arbor Rafter	6	EA
5# 16d Galv. Nails	General Framing	3	EA
5# 8d Galv. Nails	General Framing	3	EA
1# 2" Coated Screws	General Framing	2	EA
1# 2-1/2" Coated Screws	General Framing	2	EA
5# 8d Coated Box Nails	General Framing	3	EA

BENCH FRAMING

Item	Location	Qty	UM
2x4 - 6' Cedar	Bench Seat Slat	14	EA
2x4 - 8' Cedar	Seat Support	2	EA
2x6 - 8' Cedar	Seat Face Stile	4	EA

BENCH ARM & BACKREST/TRIM

Item	Location	Qty	UM
2x4 - 8' Cedar	Armrest	1	EA
1x3 - 8' Cedar	Side Rail	4	EA
2x3 - 8' Cedar	Side Rail Baluster Blocking	2	EA
1-3/8"x1-3/8"-4' Cedar	Baluster	18	EA
1x4 - 6' Cedar	Backrest	4	EA
1x8 - 6' Cedar	Lower Back Rail	4	EA
2x6 - 6' Cedar	Backrest Filler	2	EA
2x2 - 6' Cedar	Back Baluster Blocking	2	EA
2x4 - 8' Cedar	Back Baluster Blocking	2	EA
2x8 - 8' Cedar	Base Trim/Cap	8	EA
2x10 - 8' Cedar	Cap	1	EA

THE GUARDIAN

HPM-1701

This stately arbor can stand alone or attach to a fence or garden. The center gate opens to a short walkway and stands beneath a distinguished curved crown. Complete this unique and attractive arbor in a weekend and create an eye-catching focal point for your yard.

Dimensions for this arbor/gate are 10'10" X 3'11".

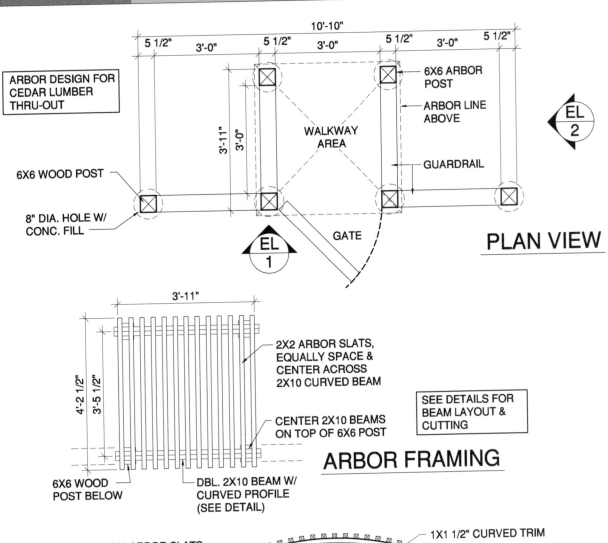

ARBOR DESIGN FOR CEDAR LUMBER THRU-OUT

10'-10"

5 1/2" 3'-0" 5 1/2" 3'-0" 5 1/2" 3'-0" 5 1/2"

6X6 ARBOR POST

ARBOR LINE ABOVE

WALKWAY AREA

3'-11" 3'-0"

GUARDRAIL

6X6 WOOD POST

8" DIA. HOLE W/ CONC. FILL

EL 1

GATE

EL 2

PLAN VIEW

3'-11"

2X2 ARBOR SLATS, EQUALLY SPACE & CENTER ACROSS 2X10 CURVED BEAM

4'-2 1/2" 3'-5 1/2"

CENTER 2X10 BEAMS ON TOP OF 6X6 POST

SEE DETAILS FOR BEAM LAYOUT & CUTTING

6X6 WOOD POST BELOW

DBL. 2X10 BEAM W/ CURVED PROFILE (SEE DETAIL)

ARBOR FRAMING

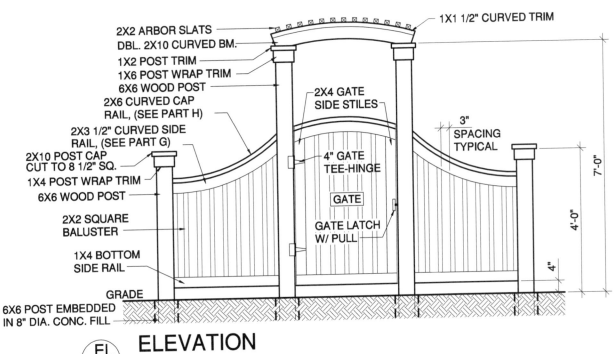

2X2 ARBOR SLATS
DBL. 2X10 CURVED BM.
1X2 POST TRIM
1X6 POST WRAP TRIM
6X6 WOOD POST
2X6 CURVED CAP RAIL, (SEE PART H)
2X3 1/2" CURVED SIDE RAIL, (SEE PART G)
2X10 POST CAP CUT TO 8 1/2" SQ.
1X4 POST WRAP TRIM
6X6 WOOD POST
2X2 SQUARE BALUSTER
1X4 BOTTOM SIDE RAIL
GRADE
6X6 POST EMBEDDED IN 8" DIA. CONC. FILL

1X1 1/2" CURVED TRIM

2X4 GATE SIDE STILES

4" GATE TEE-HINGE

GATE

GATE LATCH W/ PULL

3" SPACING TYPICAL

7'-0"

4'-0"

4"

ELEVATION

EL 1

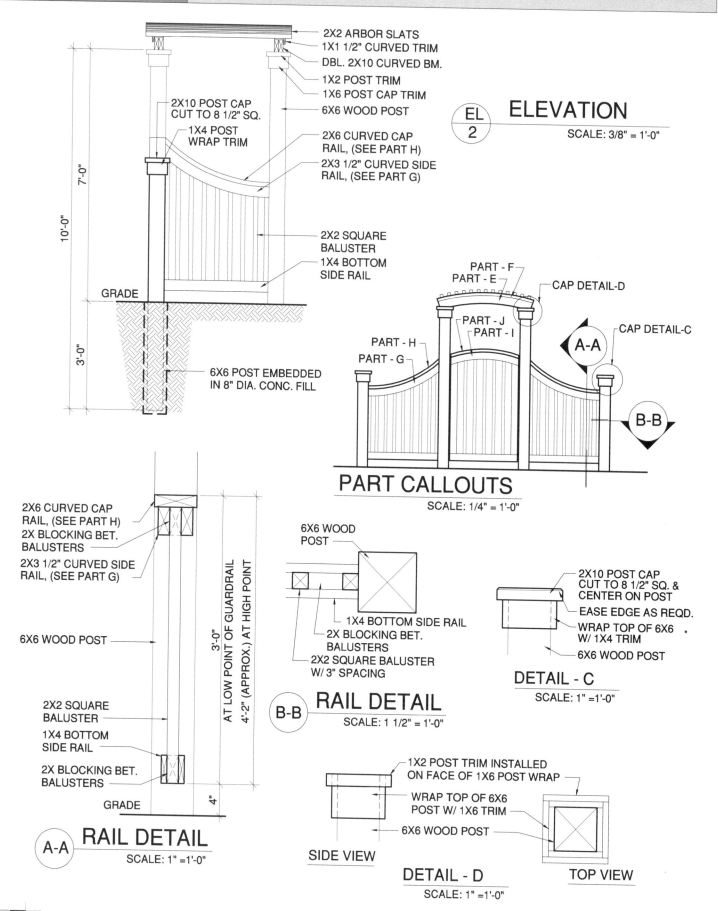

ELEVATION

2X2 ARBOR SLATS
1X1 1/2" CURVED TRIM
DBL. 2X10 CURVED BM.
1X2 POST TRIM
1X6 POST CAP TRIM
6X6 WOOD POST

2X10 POST CAP CUT TO 8 1/2" SQ.
1X4 POST WRAP TRIM

2X6 CURVED CAP RAIL, (SEE PART H)
2X3 1/2" CURVED SIDE RAIL, (SEE PART G)

2X2 SQUARE BALUSTER
1X4 BOTTOM SIDE RAIL

GRADE

6X6 POST EMBEDDED IN 8" DIA. CONC. FILL

7'-0"
10'-0"
3'-0"

EL 2 — **ELEVATION**
SCALE: 3/8" = 1'-0"

PART - F
PART - E
CAP DETAIL-D

PART - J
PART - I
CAP DETAIL-C

PART - H
PART - G

A-A
B-B

PART CALLOUTS
SCALE: 1/4" = 1'-0"

2X6 CURVED CAP RAIL, (SEE PART H)
2X BLOCKING BET. BALUSTERS
2X3 1/2" CURVED SIDE RAIL, (SEE PART G)

6X6 WOOD POST

2X2 SQUARE BALUSTER
1X4 BOTTOM SIDE RAIL
2X BLOCKING BET. BALUSTERS

GRADE

3'-0"
AT LOW POINT OF GUARDRAIL
4'-2" (APPROX.) AT HIGH POINT
4"

A-A — **RAIL DETAIL**
SCALE: 1" =1'-0"

6X6 WOOD POST

1X4 BOTTOM SIDE RAIL
2X BLOCKING BET. BALUSTERS
2X2 SQUARE BALUSTER W/ 3" SPACING

B-B — **RAIL DETAIL**
SCALE: 1 1/2" = 1'-0"

2X10 POST CAP CUT TO 8 1/2" SQ. & CENTER ON POST
EASE EDGE AS REQD.
WRAP TOP OF 6X6 W/ 1X4 TRIM
6X6 WOOD POST

DETAIL - C
SCALE: 1" =1'-0"

1X2 POST TRIM INSTALLED ON FACE OF 1X6 POST WRAP
WRAP TOP OF 6X6 POST W/ 1X6 TRIM
6X6 WOOD POST

SIDE VIEW
TOP VIEW

DETAIL - D
SCALE: 1" =1'-0"

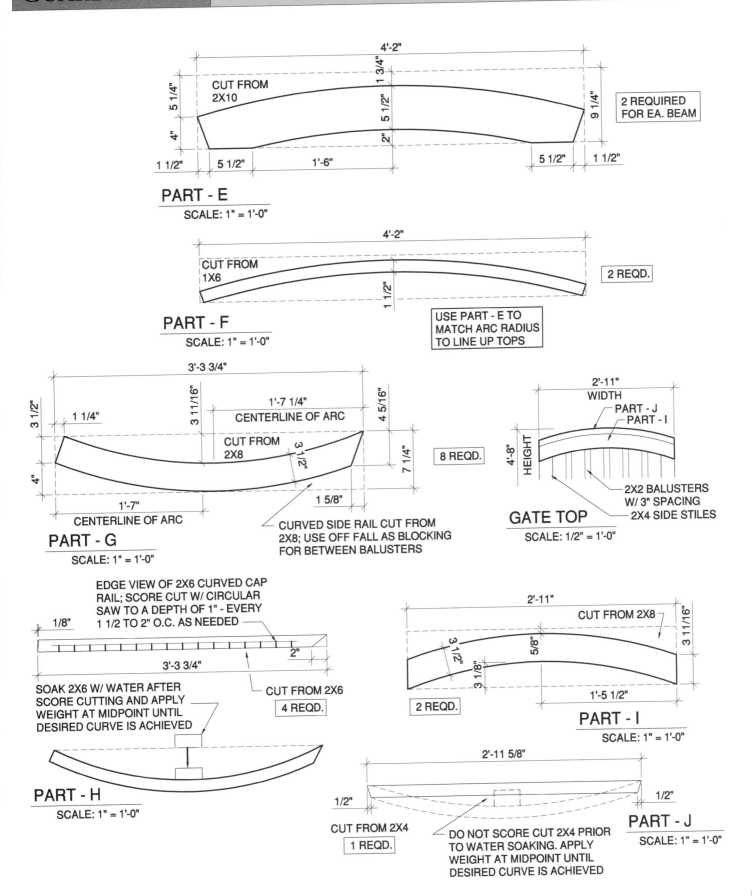

4'-2"

5 1/4"
1 3/4"
5 1/2"
4"
2"

CUT FROM
2X10

9 1/4"

2 REQUIRED
FOR EA. BEAM

1 1/2"   5 1/2"   1'-6"   5 1/2"   1 1/2"

PART - E
SCALE: 1" = 1'-0"

4'-2"

CUT FROM
1X6

1 1/2"

2 REQD.

USE PART - E TO
MATCH ARC RADIUS
TO LINE UP TOPS

PART - F
SCALE: 1" = 1'-0"

3'-3 3/4"

3 1/2"
1 1/4"
3 11/16"
1'-7 1/4"
CENTERLINE OF ARC
4 5/16"

CUT FROM
2X8
3 1/2"

4"
7 1/4"

8 REQD.

1'-7"
CENTERLINE OF ARC

1 5/8"

CURVED SIDE RAIL CUT FROM
2X8; USE OFF FALL AS BLOCKING
FOR BETWEEN BALUSTERS

PART - G
SCALE: 1" = 1'-0"

2'-11"
WIDTH
PART - J
PART - I

4'-8"
HEIGHT

2X2 BALUSTERS
W/ 3" SPACING
2X4 SIDE STILES

GATE TOP
SCALE: 1/2" = 1'-0"

EDGE VIEW OF 2X6 CURVED CAP
RAIL; SCORE CUT W/ CIRCULAR
SAW TO A DEPTH OF 1" - EVERY
1 1/2 TO 2" O.C. AS NEEDED

1/8"
2"
3'-3 3/4"

SOAK 2X6 W/ WATER AFTER
SCORE CUTTING AND APPLY
WEIGHT AT MIDPOINT UNTIL
DESIRED CURVE IS ACHIEVED

CUT FROM 2X6
4 REQD.

PART - H
SCALE: 1" = 1'-0"

2'-11"
CUT FROM 2X8
3 11/16"
3 1/2"
5/8"
3 1/8"
1'-5 1/2"

2 REQD.

PART - I
SCALE: 1" = 1'-0"

2'-11 5/8"

1/2"
1/2"

CUT FROM 2X4
1 REQD.

DO NOT SCORE CUT 2X4 PRIOR
TO WATER SOAKING. APPLY
WEIGHT AT MIDPOINT UNTIL
DESIRED CURVE IS ACHIEVED

PART - J
SCALE: 1" = 1'-0"

ARBOR GATE FRAMING

Item	Location	Qty	UM
60# Concrete Mix	Post	12	BG
6x6 - 10' Cedar	Post	4	EA
6x6 - 8' Cedar	Post	2	EA
2x10 - 10' Cedar	Beam	2	EA
2x2 - 10' Cedar	Arbor Slat	7	EA
5# 16d Galv. Nails	General Framing	3	EA
5# 8d Galv. Nails	General Framing	3	EA
1# 2" Coated Screws	General Framing	2	EA
1# 2-1/2" Coated Screws	General Framing	2	EA
5# 8d Coated Box Nails	General Framing	3	EA

GATE/ARBOR RAILING

Item	Location	Qty	UM
2x4 - 6' Cedar	Gate - Blstr. Blkg./Part (J)	2	EA
2x4 - 8' Cedar	Arbor Baluster Blocking	3	EA
2x6 - 8' Cedar	Arbor Part (H)	2	EA
2x8 - 6' Cedar	Gate Part (I)	1	EA
2x8 - 8' Cedar	Arbor Part (G)	4	EA
1x4 - 6' Cedar	Arbor/Gate Bottom Side Rail	5	EA
2x2 - 10' Cedar	Arbor/Gate Baluster	21	EA
Gate Hardware Kit	Gate	1	EA

TRIM

Item	Location	Qty	UM
1x6 - 10' Cedar	Beam Trim Part (F)	1	EA
1x6 - 8' Cedar	Post Wrap Detail (D)	2	EA
1x2 - 8' Cedar	Post Trim Detail (D)	2	EA
1x4' - 8' Cedar	Post Wrap Detail (C)	1	EA
1x2 - 8' Cedar	Post Trim Detail (C)	1	EA
2x10 - 6' Cedar	Post Cap	1	EA

THE TRADITIONAL   HPM-1704
Dimensions for this fence section are 5' X 6'.

THE TRADITIONAL & EUROSTYLE

Protect your small children and pets with attractive fencing that complements the style of your home. Surround your yard with the simple lines of this traditional fence that will never look outdated.

Adding a row of lattice creates a charming European flair, as illustrated by the Eurostyle fence below. While this fence is two feet higher, the lattice lets in light and imparts an open feel.

THE EUROSTYLE   HPM-1705
Dimensions for this fence section are 7' X 6'.

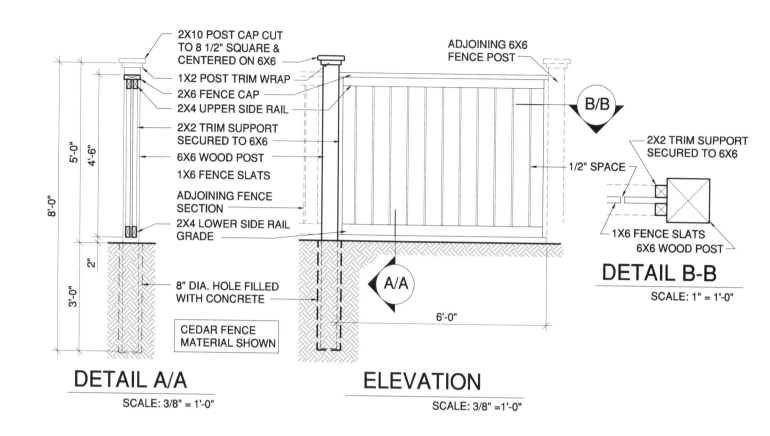

DETAIL A/A
SCALE: 3/8" = 1'-0"

ELEVATION
SCALE: 3/8" =1'-0"

DETAIL B-B
SCALE: 1" = 1'-0"

FENCE (6'-0" SECTION)

Item	Location	Qty	UM
60# Concrete Mix	Post	2	BG
6x6 - 8' Cedar	Post	1	EA
2x6 - 6' Cedar (Cut to 5'6-1/2")	Panel Cap	1	EA
2x4 - 6' Cedar (Cut to 5'6-1/2")	Side Rail	4	EA
2x2 - 6' Cedar (Cut to 4'4-1/2")	Support	4	EA
1x6 - 6' Cedar (Cut to 4'4-1/2")	Slat	12	EA
1x2 - 6' Cedar (Cut to 7")	Trim	1	EA
2x10 - 6' Cedar (Cut to 8-1/2"x8-1/2")	Post Cap	1	EA
1# 2-1/2" Coated Screws	General Framing	3	EA
1# 4d Coated Box Nails	General Framing	1	EA

FENCE TERMINATION MATERIAL

Item	Location	Qty	UM
60# Concrete Mix	Post	2	BG
6x6 - 8' Cedar	Post	1	EA
2x10 - 6' Cedar (Cut to 8-1/2"x8-1/2")	Post Cap	1	EA
1x2 - 6' Cedar (Cut to 7")	Trim	1	EA

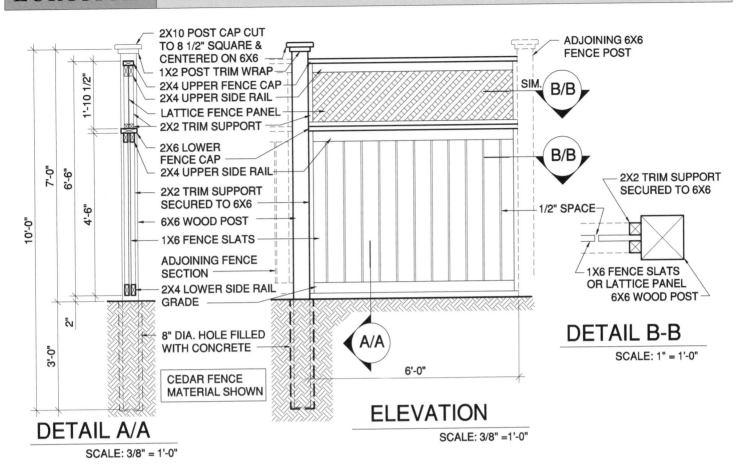

DETAIL A/A
SCALE: 3/8" = 1'-0"

- 2X10 POST CAP CUT TO 8 1/2" SQUARE & CENTERED ON 6X6
- 1X2 POST TRIM WRAP
- 2X4 UPPER FENCE CAP
- 2X4 UPPER SIDE RAIL
- LATTICE FENCE PANEL
- 2X2 TRIM SUPPORT
- 2X6 LOWER FENCE CAP
- 2X4 UPPER SIDE RAIL
- 2X2 TRIM SUPPORT SECURED TO 6X6
- 6X6 WOOD POST
- 1X6 FENCE SLATS
- ADJOINING FENCE SECTION
- 2X4 LOWER SIDE RAIL
- GRADE
- 8" DIA. HOLE FILLED WITH CONCRETE
- CEDAR FENCE MATERIAL SHOWN

ADJOINING 6X6 FENCE POST

SIM. B/B

B/B

ELEVATION
SCALE: 3/8" =1'-0"

DETAIL B-B
SCALE: 1" = 1'-0"

- 2X2 TRIM SUPPORT SECURED TO 6X6
- 1/2" SPACE
- 1X6 FENCE SLATS OR LATTICE PANEL
- 6X6 WOOD POST

EUROSTYLE — Material List

FENCE (6'-0" SECTION)

Item	Location	Qty	UM
60# Concrete Mix	Post	2	BG
6x6 - 10' Cedar	Post	1	EA
2x4 - 6' Cedar (Cut to 5'6-1/2")	Upper Cap	1	EA
2x6 - 6' Cedar (Cut to 5'6-1/2")	Lower Cap	1	EA
2x4 - 6' Cedar (Cut to 5'3-1/2")	Side Rail	6	EA
2x2 - 6' Cedar (Cut to 5'6-1/2")	Trim Support	2	EA
2x2 - 6' Cedar (Cut to 4'6")	Support	4	EA
2x2 - 8' Cedar (Cut to 1'10-1/2")	Trim Support	1	EA
1x6 - 6' Cedar (Cut to 4'6")	Slat	12	EA
1x2 - 6' Cedar (Cut to 7")	Trim	1	EA
2x10 - 6' Cedar (Cut to 8-1/2"x8-1/2")	Post Cap	1	EA
Cedar Lattice	Panel	1	EA
1# 2-1/2" Coated Screws	General Framing	5	EA
1# 4d Coated Box Nails	General Framing	1	EA

FENCE TERMINATION MATERIAL

Item	Location	Qty	UM
60# Concrete Mix	Post	2	BG
6x6 - 10' Cedar	Post	1	EA
2x10 - 6' Cedar (Cut to 8-1/2"x8-1/2")	Post Cap	1	EA
1x2 - 6' Cedar (Cut to 7")	Trim	1	EA

THE COUNTRY   **HPM-1706**

Dimensions for this fence section are 5' X 6'.

THE COUNTRY & CONTEMPO

Pointed fence slats create the picket fence you've always dreamed of. Paint the fence white for a cottage look or keep the wood natural with a clear or tinted stain.

Alternating the fence slats on either side of the rails offers a contemporary look. The Contempo fence shown below has extra-long slats and is ideal for surrounding a pool or creating a privacy barrier.

THE CONTEMPO   **HPM-1707**

Dimensions for this fence section are 7' X 12'.

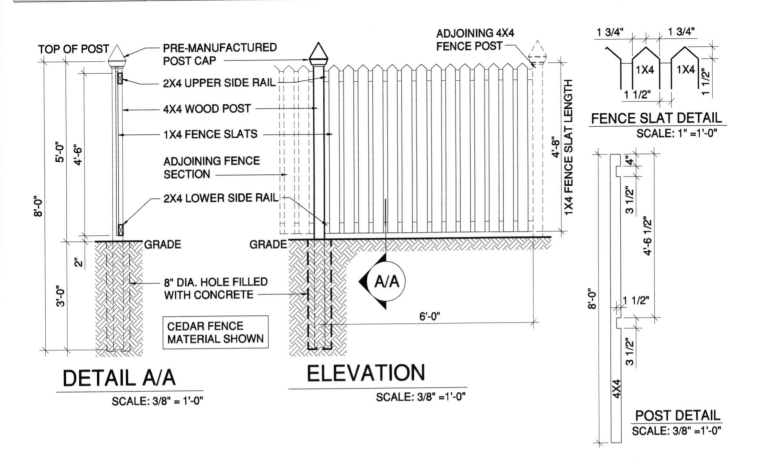

DETAIL A/A
SCALE: 3/8" = 1'-0"

ELEVATION
SCALE: 3/8" =1'-0"

FENCE SLAT DETAIL
SCALE: 1" =1'-0"

POST DETAIL
SCALE: 3/8" =1'-0"

COUNTRY | Material List

FENCE (6'-0" SECTION)

Item	Location	Qty	UM
60# Concrete Mix	Post	2	BG
4x4 - 8' Cedar	Post	1	EA
2x4 - 6' Cedar	Upper/Lower Cap	2	EA
1x4 - 6' Cedar	Slat	14	EA
Pre-Manufactured Post Cap	Post	1	EA
1# 2" Coated Screws	General Framing	5	EA
1# 2-1/2" Coated Screws	General Framing	1	EA

FENCE TERMINATION MATERIAL

Item	Location	Qty	UM
60# Concrete Mix	Post	2	BG
4x4 - 8' Cedar	Post	1	EA
Pre-Manufactured Post Cap	Post	1	EA

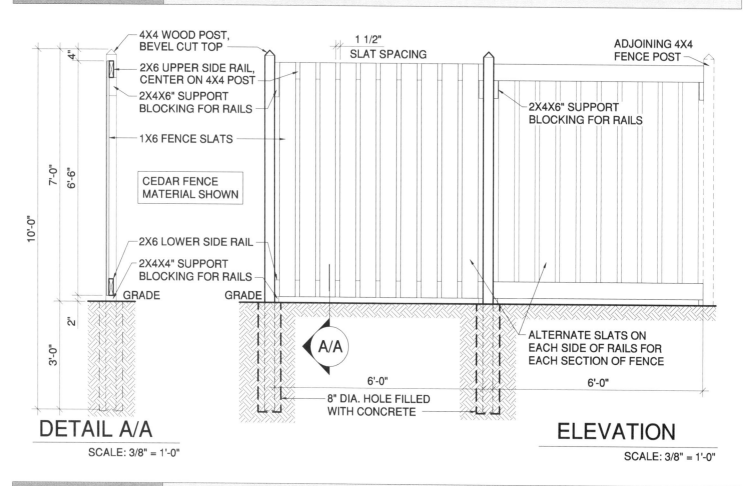

DETAIL A/A
SCALE: 3/8" = 1'-0"

ELEVATION
SCALE: 3/8" = 1'-0"

CONTEMPO Material List

FENCE (12'-0" SECTION)

Item	Location	Qty	UM
60# Concrete Mix	Post	4	BG
4x4 - 10' Cedar	Post	2	EA
2x4 - 6' Cedar (4) - 4" (4) - 6"	Rail Block	1	EA
2x6 -6' Cedar (Cut to 5'8-1/2")	Top/Bottom Rail	4	EA
1x6 - 8' Cedar (Cut to 6'6")	Slat	20	EA
1# 1-5/8" Coated Screws	General Framing	5	EA
1# 2-1/2" Coated Screws	General Framing	1	EA

FENCE TERMINATION MATERIAL

Item	Location	Qty	UM
60# Concrete Mix	Post	2	BG
4x4 - 10' Cedar	Post	1	EA

THE PINEHILL   HPM-1716
Dimensions for this chair are 1'10" X 1'4".

THE PINEHILL & ASHVILLE

Unique and adaptable to any style, this durable chair will look great on your deck, patio or porch. Add a cushion for added comfort and appeal. Customize the chair with paint or a wood finish to complement your home or other outdoor furniture.

Add romance and charm to your deck or patio by grouping the chair with this outdoor bench. There's room for your own design flair, as well as your favorite companion. With its sunburst detailing, it complements the flower and window boxes you can build to match.

THE ASHVILLE   HPM-1717
Dimensions for this bench are 4' X 1'6".

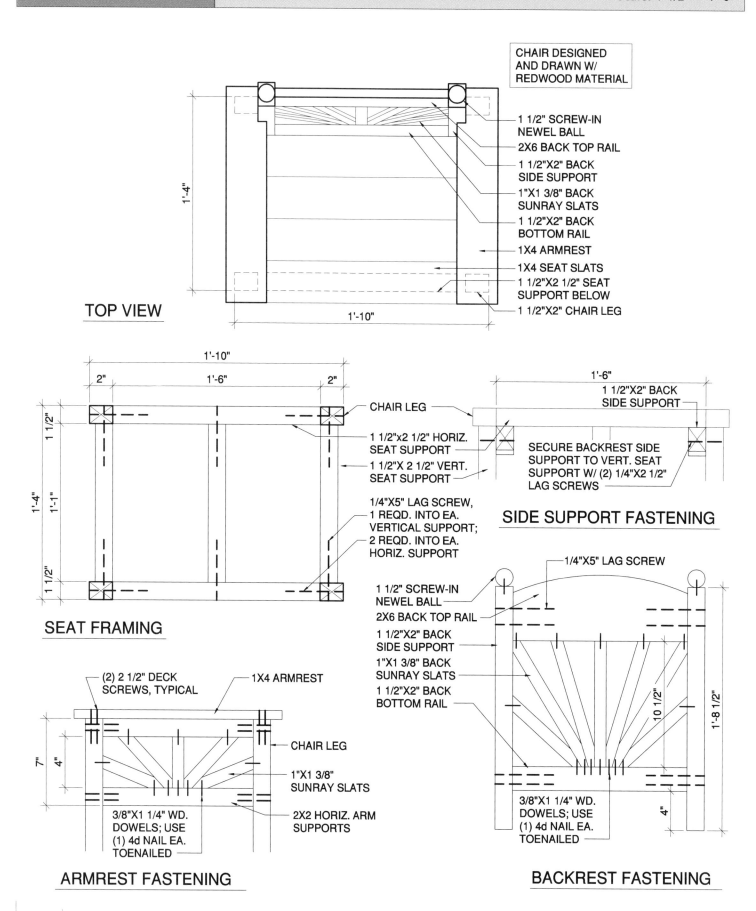

CHAIR DESIGNED
AND DRAWN W/
REDWOOD MATERIAL

TOP VIEW

1'-4"

1'-10"

1 1/2" SCREW-IN
NEWEL BALL

2X6 BACK TOP RAIL

1 1/2"X2" BACK
SIDE SUPPORT

1"X1 3/8" BACK
SUNRAY SLATS

1 1/2"X2" BACK
BOTTOM RAIL

1X4 ARMREST

1X4 SEAT SLATS

1 1/2"X2 1/2" SEAT
SUPPORT BELOW

1 1/2"X2" CHAIR LEG

SEAT FRAMING

1'-10"

2"   1'-6"   2"

1 1/2"

1'-4"   1'-1"

1 1/2"

CHAIR LEG

1 1/2"x2 1/2" HORIZ.
SEAT SUPPORT

1 1/2"X 2 1/2" VERT.
SEAT SUPPORT

1/4"X5" LAG SCREW,
1 REQD. INTO EA.
VERTICAL SUPPORT;
2 REQD. INTO EA.
HORIZ. SUPPORT

SIDE SUPPORT FASTENING

1'-6"

1 1/2"X2" BACK
SIDE SUPPORT

SECURE BACKREST SIDE
SUPPORT TO VERT. SEAT
SUPPORT W/ (2) 1/4"X2 1/2"
LAG SCREWS

ARMREST FASTENING

(2) 2 1/2" DECK
SCREWS, TYPICAL

1X4 ARMREST

7"   4"

CHAIR LEG

1"X1 3/8"
SUNRAY SLATS

3/8"X1 1/4" WD.
DOWELS; USE
(1) 4d NAIL EA.
TOENAILED

2X2 HORIZ. ARM
SUPPORTS

BACKREST FASTENING

1/4"X5" LAG SCREW

1 1/2" SCREW-IN
NEWEL BALL

2X6 BACK TOP RAIL

1 1/2"X2" BACK
SIDE SUPPORT

1"X1 3/8" BACK
SUNRAY SLATS

1 1/2"X2" BACK
BOTTOM RAIL

10 1/2"

1'-8 1/2"

4"

3/8"X1 1/4" WD.
DOWELS; USE
(1) 4d NAIL EA.
TOENAILED

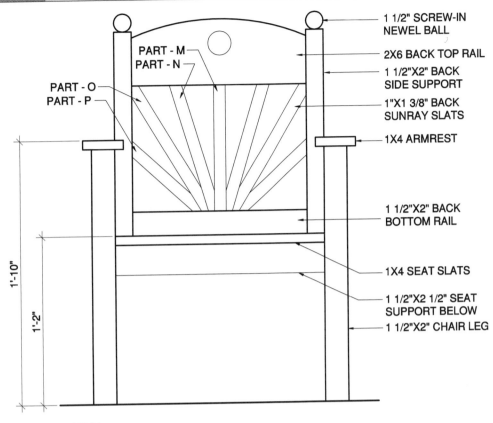

PART - M
PART - N

PART - O
PART - P

1 1/2" SCREW-IN
NEWEL BALL

2X6 BACK TOP RAIL

1 1/2"X2" BACK
SIDE SUPPORT

1"X1 3/8" BACK
SUNRAY SLATS

1X4 ARMREST

1 1/2"X2" BACK
BOTTOM RAIL

1X4 SEAT SLATS

1 1/2"X2 1/2" SEAT
SUPPORT BELOW

1 1/2"X2" CHAIR LEG

1'-10"

1'-2"

FRONT VIEW

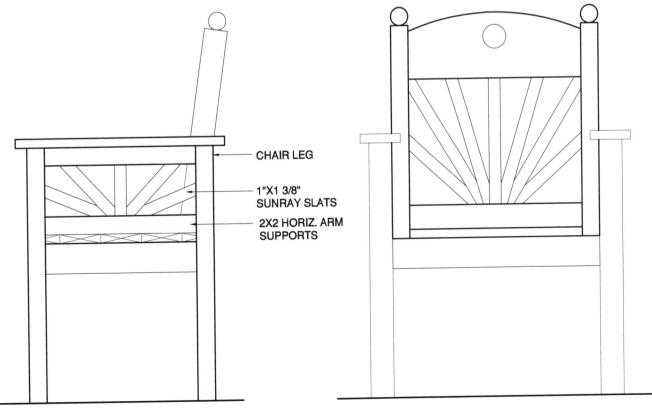

CHAIR LEG

1"X1 3/8"
SUNRAY SLATS

2X2 HORIZ. ARM
SUPPORTS

SIDE VIEW

BACK VIEW

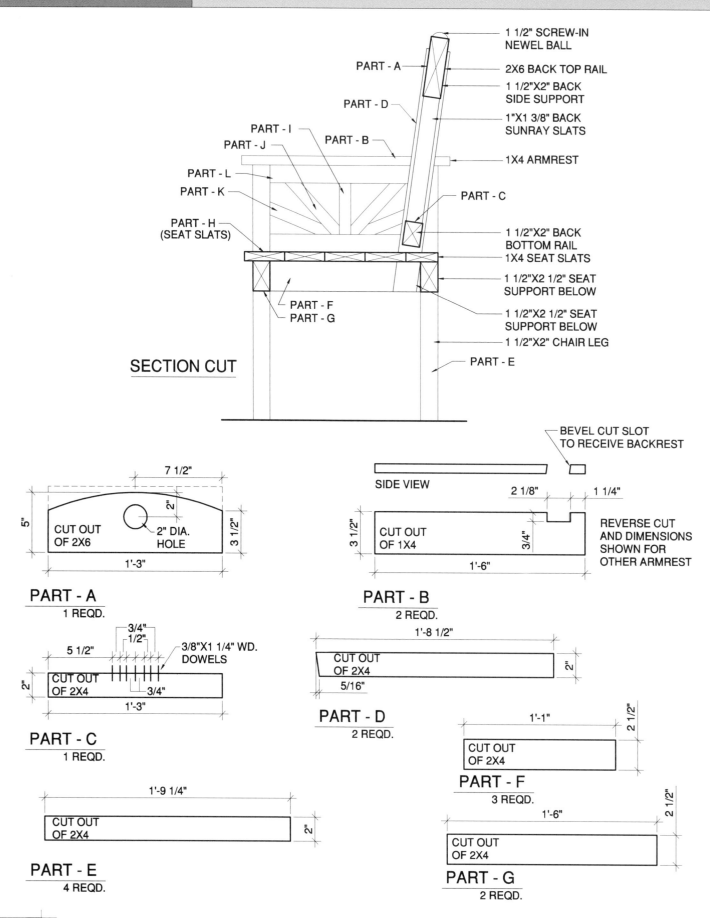

1 1/2" SCREW-IN
NEWEL BALL

PART - A — 2X6 BACK TOP RAIL

1 1/2"X2" BACK
SIDE SUPPORT

PART - D

1"X1 3/8" BACK
SUNRAY SLATS

PART - I
PART - J
PART - B — 1X4 ARMREST

PART - L

PART - K

PART - C

PART - H
(SEAT SLATS) — 1 1/2"X2" BACK
BOTTOM RAIL

1X4 SEAT SLATS

1 1/2"X2 1/2" SEAT
SUPPORT BELOW

PART - F
PART - G — 1 1/2"X2 1/2" SEAT
SUPPORT BELOW

1 1/2"X2" CHAIR LEG

PART - E

SECTION CUT

PART - A
1 REQD.

7 1/2"
5"
2"
3 1/2"
CUT OUT
OF 2X6
2" DIA.
HOLE
1'-3"

PART - B
2 REQD.

BEVEL CUT SLOT
TO RECEIVE BACKREST

SIDE VIEW

2 1/8"   1 1/4"

3 1/2"
CUT OUT
OF 1X4
3/4"
REVERSE CUT
AND DIMENSIONS
SHOWN FOR
OTHER ARMREST
1'-6"

PART - C
1 REQD.

3/4"
1/2"
3/8"X1 1/4" WD.
DOWELS
5 1/2"
2"
CUT OUT
OF 2X4
3/4"
1'-3"

PART - D
2 REQD.

1'-8 1/2"
CUT OUT
OF 2X4
2"
5/16"

PART - F
3 REQD.

1'-1"
2 1/2"
CUT OUT
OF 2X4

PART - E
4 REQD.

1'-9 1/4"
CUT OUT
OF 2X4
2"

PART - G
2 REQD.

1'-6"
2 1/2"
CUT OUT
OF 2X4

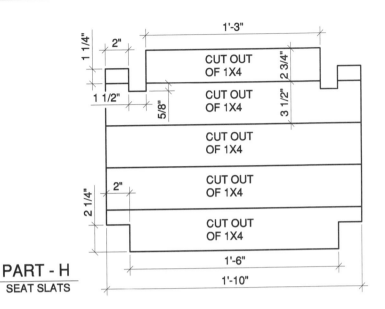

PART - H
SEAT SLATS

CUT OUT OF 1X4

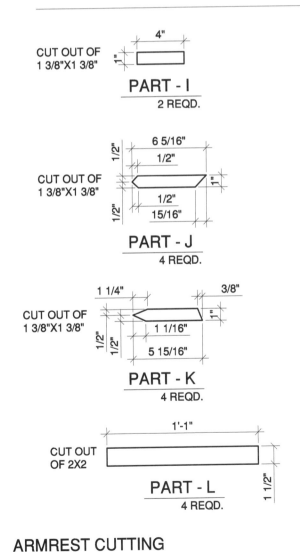

CUT OUT OF 1 3/8"X1 3/8"
PART - I
2 REQD.

CUT OUT OF 1 3/8"X1 3/8"
PART - J
4 REQD.

CUT OUT OF 1 3/8"X1 3/8"
PART - K
4 REQD.

CUT OUT OF 2X2
PART - L
4 REQD.

ARMREST CUTTING

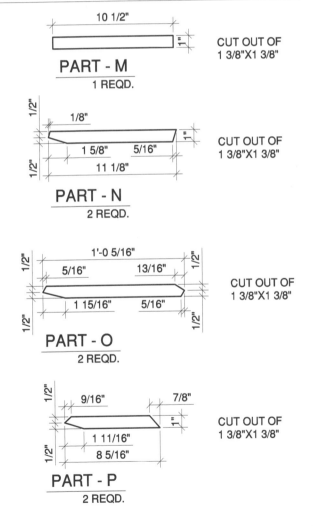

CUT OUT OF 1 3/8"X1 3/8"
PART - M
1 REQD.

CUT OUT OF 1 3/8"X1 3/8"
PART - N
2 REQD.

CUT OUT OF 1 3/8"X1 3/8"
PART - O
2 REQD.

CUT OUT OF 1 3/8"X1 3/8"
PART - P
2 REQD.

BACKREST CUTTING

CHAIR

Item	Location	Qty	UM
2x4 - 8' Redwood	Parts C/D/E/F/G	3	EA
2x2 - 8' Redwood	Part L	1	EA
1x4 - 8' Redwood	Parts B/H	2	EA
1-3/8"x1-3/8" -8' Redwood	Parts I/J/K/M/N/O/P	2	EA
3/8" - 36" Wood Dowel	Sunray Slat	2	EA
1-1/2" Dia. Newel Ball w/Screw	Corner Post	2	EA
2x6 - 6' Redwood	Part A	1	EA
1/4"x2-1/2" Lag Screw	General Framing	8	EA
1/4"x5" Lag Screws	General Framing	20	EA
5# 2-1/2" Coated Screws	General Framing	1	EA
1# 4d Coated Box Nails	General Framing	1	EA

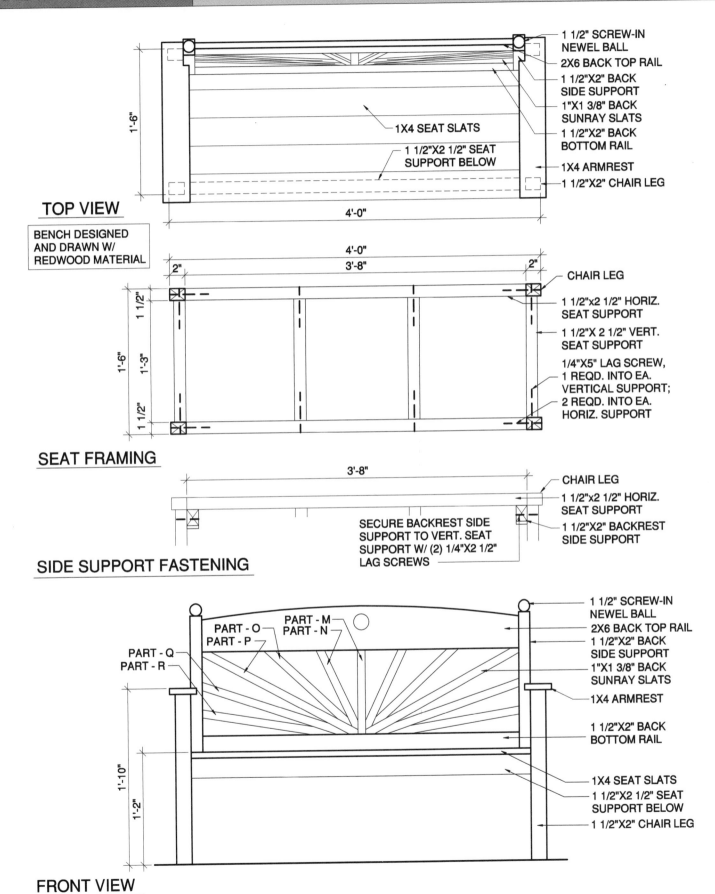

TOP VIEW

1 1/2" SCREW-IN NEWEL BALL
2X6 BACK TOP RAIL
1 1/2"X2" BACK SIDE SUPPORT
1"X1 3/8" BACK SUNRAY SLATS
1 1/2"X2" BACK BOTTOM RAIL
1X4 ARMREST
1 1/2"X2" CHAIR LEG

1X4 SEAT SLATS
1 1/2"X2 1/2" SEAT SUPPORT BELOW

1'-6"
4'-0"

BENCH DESIGNED AND DRAWN W/ REDWOOD MATERIAL

SEAT FRAMING

4'-0"
3'-8"
2"   2"

CHAIR LEG
1 1/2"x2 1/2" HORIZ. SEAT SUPPORT
1 1/2"X 2 1/2" VERT. SEAT SUPPORT
1/4"X5" LAG SCREW, 1 REQD. INTO EA. VERTICAL SUPPORT; 2 REQD. INTO EA. HORIZ. SUPPORT

1 1/2"
1'-6"
1'-3"
1 1/2"

SIDE SUPPORT FASTENING

3'-8"

CHAIR LEG
1 1/2"x2 1/2" HORIZ. SEAT SUPPORT
1 1/2"X2" BACKREST SIDE SUPPORT

SECURE BACKREST SIDE SUPPORT TO VERT. SEAT SUPPORT W/ (2) 1/4"X2 1/2" LAG SCREWS

FRONT VIEW

PART - O
PART - P
PART - M
PART - N
PART - Q
PART - R

1 1/2" SCREW-IN NEWEL BALL
2X6 BACK TOP RAIL
1 1/2"X2" BACK SIDE SUPPORT
1"X1 3/8" BACK SUNRAY SLATS
1X4 ARMREST
1 1/2"X2" BACK BOTTOM RAIL
1X4 SEAT SLATS
1 1/2"X2 1/2" SEAT SUPPORT BELOW
1 1/2"X2" CHAIR LEG

1'-10"
1'-2"

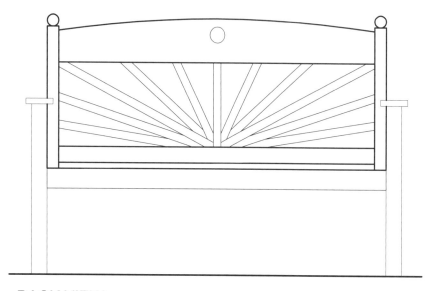

BACK VIEW

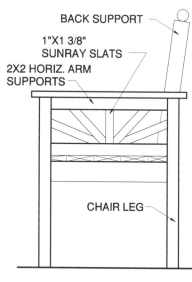

BACK SUPPORT

1"X1 3/8"
SUNRAY SLATS

2X2 HORIZ. ARM
SUPPORTS

CHAIR LEG

SIDE VIEW

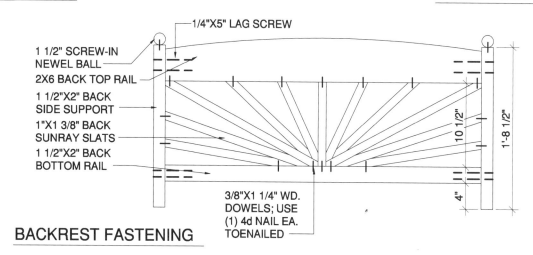

1/4"X5" LAG SCREW

1 1/2" SCREW-IN
NEWEL BALL

2X6 BACK TOP RAIL

1 1/2"X2" BACK
SIDE SUPPORT

1"X1 3/8" BACK
SUNRAY SLATS

1 1/2"X2" BACK
BOTTOM RAIL

3/8"X1 1/4" WD.
DOWELS; USE
(1) 4d NAIL EA.
TOENAILED

10 1/2"

1'-8 1/2"

4"

BACKREST FASTENING

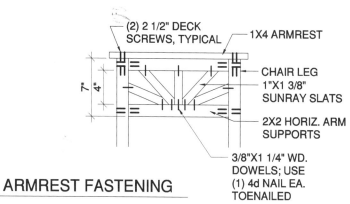

(2) 2 1/2" DECK
SCREWS, TYPICAL

1X4 ARMREST

CHAIR LEG

1"X1 3/8"
SUNRAY SLATS

2X2 HORIZ. ARM
SUPPORTS

3/8"X1 1/4" WD.
DOWELS; USE
(1) 4d NAIL EA.
TOENAILED

7"

4"

ARMREST FASTENING

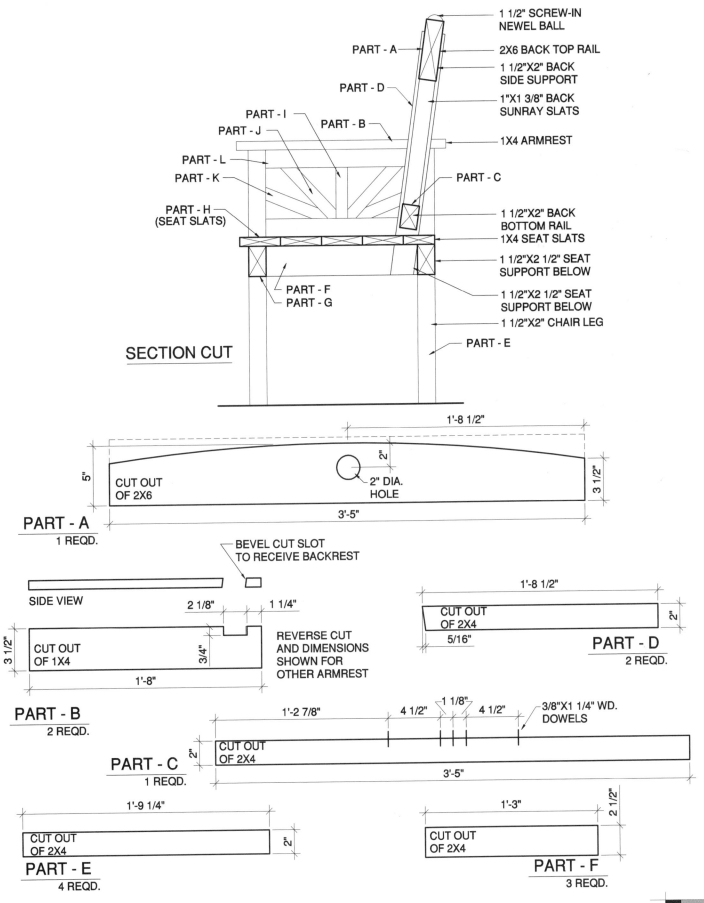

SECTION CUT

1 1/2" SCREW-IN NEWEL BALL

PART - A

2X6 BACK TOP RAIL

PART - D

1 1/2"X2" BACK SIDE SUPPORT

1"X1 3/8" BACK SUNRAY SLATS

PART - I
PART - J
PART - B

1X4 ARMREST

PART - L
PART - K

PART - C

PART - H
(SEAT SLATS)

1 1/2"X2" BACK BOTTOM RAIL
1X4 SEAT SLATS

PART - F
PART - G

1 1/2"X2 1/2" SEAT SUPPORT BELOW

1 1/2"X2 1/2" SEAT SUPPORT BELOW

1 1/2"X2" CHAIR LEG

PART - E

PART - A

1 REQD.

1'-8 1/2"
5"
3 1/2"
3'-5"
2"
2" DIA. HOLE

CUT OUT OF 2X6

PART - B

2 REQD.

SIDE VIEW

BEVEL CUT SLOT TO RECEIVE BACKREST

CUT OUT OF 1X4

3 1/2"
1'-8"
2 1/8"
1 1/4"
3/4"

REVERSE CUT AND DIMENSIONS SHOWN FOR OTHER ARMREST

PART - C

1 REQD.

CUT OUT OF 2X4

2"
1'-2 7/8"
4 1/2"
1 1/8"
4 1/2"
3/8"X1 1/4" WD. DOWELS
3'-5"

PART - D

2 REQD.

1'-8 1/2"
CUT OUT OF 2X4
2"
5/16"

PART - E

4 REQD.

1'-9 1/4"
CUT OUT OF 2X4
2"

PART - F

3 REQD.

1'-3"
CUT OUT OF 2X4
2 1/2"

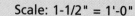

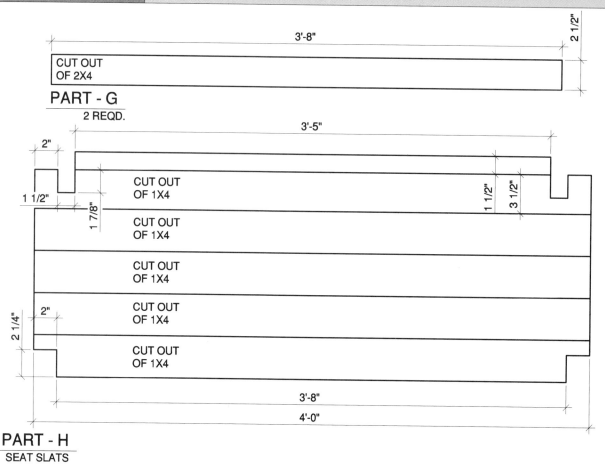

PART - G
2 REQD.

CUT OUT OF 2X4

3'-8"

2 1/2"

PART - H
SEAT SLATS

CUT OUT OF 1X4

3'-5"

2"

1 1/2"

1 7/8"

1 1/2"

3 1/2"

2 1/4"

2"

3'-8"

4'-0"

ARMREST CUTTING

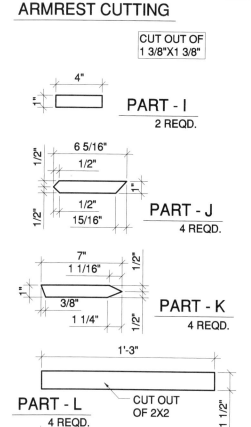

CUT OUT OF 1 3/8"X1 3/8"

PART - I
2 REQD.

4"

1"

PART - J
4 REQD.

6 5/16"

1/2"

1/2"

1/2"

15/16"

1"

PART - K
4 REQD.

7"

1 1/16"

1/2"

3/8"

1 1/4"

1"

1/2"

PART - L
4 REQD.

1'-3"

CUT OUT OF 2X2

1 1/2"

BACKREST CUTTING

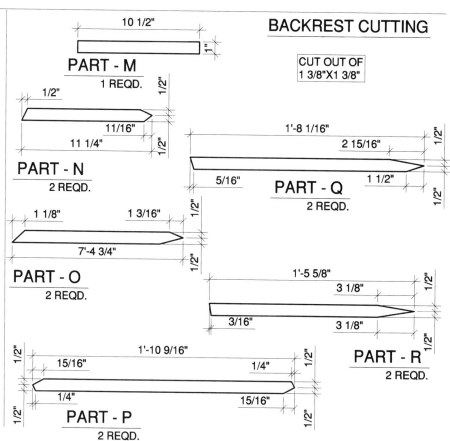

CUT OUT OF 1 3/8"X1 3/8"

PART - M
1 REQD.

10 1/2"

1"

1/2"

PART - N
2 REQD.

1/2"

1/2"

11/16"

1/2"

11 1/4"

PART - O
2 REQD.

1 1/8"

1 3/16"

1/2"

7'-4 3/4"

1/2"

PART - Q
2 REQD.

1'-8 1/16"

2 15/16"

1/2"

5/16"

1 1/2"

1/2"

PART - R
2 REQD.

1'-5 5/8"

3 1/8"

1/2"

3/16"

3 1/8"

1/2"

PART - P
2 REQD.

1'-10 9/16"

1/2"

15/16"

1/4"

1/2"

1/4"

15/16"

1/2"

BENCH

Item	Location	Qty	UM
2x4 - 8' Redwood	Parts C/D/E/F/G	4	EA
2x2 - 8' Redwood	Part L	1	EA
1x4 - 8' Redwood	Parts B/H	3	EA
1-3/8"x1-3/8" -8' Redwood	Parts I/J/K/M/N/O/P/Q/R	3	EA
3/8" - 36" Wood Dowel	Sunray Slat	2	EA
1-1/2" Dia. Newel Ball w/Screw	Corner Post	2	EA
2x6 - 6' Redwood	Part A	1	EA
1/4"x2-1/2" Lag Screw	General Framing	8	EA
1/4"x5" Lag Screw	General Framing	20	EA
5# 2-1/2" Coated Screws	General Framing	1	EA
1# 4d Coated Box Nails	General Framing	1	EA

THE SUMMERVILLE

HPM-1710

With its open octagonal design, this picnic table can comfortably seat eight people. Its shape also lends itself to easier food service and conversation. Drill a hole in the center and add an umbrella for relief from the sun.

Dimensions for this picnic table are 6'11" X 6'11".

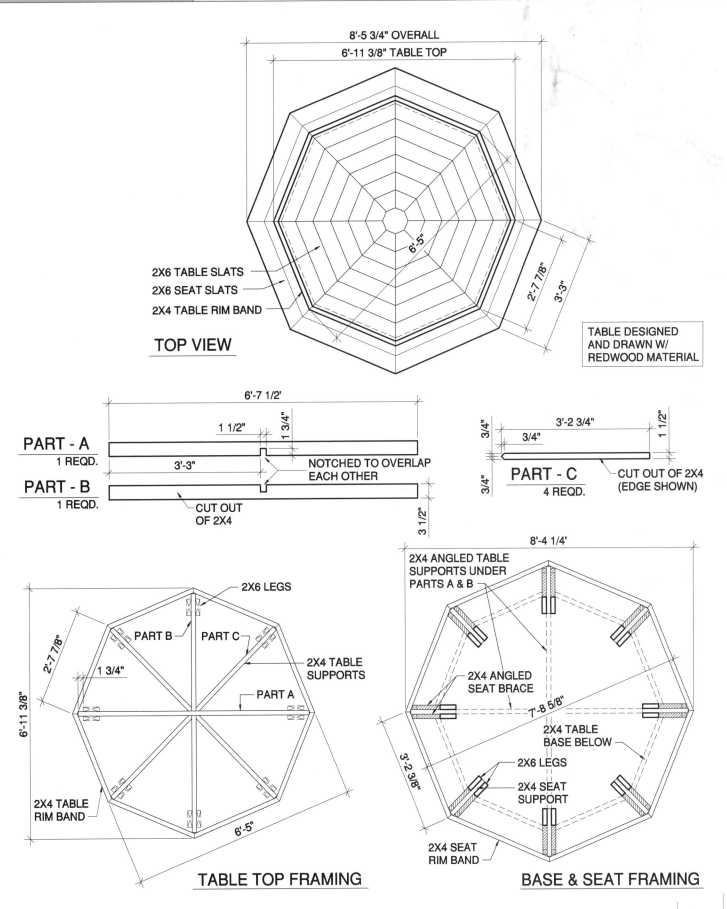

8'-5 3/4" OVERALL
6'-11 3/8" TABLE TOP
6'-5"
2'-7 7/8"
3'-3"

2X6 TABLE SLATS
2X6 SEAT SLATS
2X4 TABLE RIM BAND

TOP VIEW

TABLE DESIGNED
AND DRAWN W/
REDWOOD MATERIAL

PART - A
1 REQD.

PART - B
1 REQD.

6'-7 1/2'
1 1/2"
1 3/4"
3'-3"
3 1/2"

NOTCHED TO OVERLAP
EACH OTHER

CUT OUT
OF 2X4

PART - C
4 REQD.

3/4"
3'-2 3/4"
3/4"
1 1/2"
3/4"

CUT OUT OF 2X4
(EDGE SHOWN)

2X6 LEGS
PART B   PART C
2'-7 7/8"
1 3/4"
6'-11 3/8"
PART A
2X4 TABLE
SUPPORTS
2X4 TABLE
RIM BAND
6'-5"

TABLE TOP FRAMING

8'-4 1/4'
2X4 ANGLED TABLE
SUPPORTS UNDER
PARTS A & B
2X4 ANGLED
SEAT BRACE
7'-8 5/8"
2X4 TABLE
BASE BELOW
3'-2 3/8"
2X6 LEGS
2X4 SEAT
SUPPORT
2X4 SEAT
RIM BAND

BASE & SEAT FRAMING

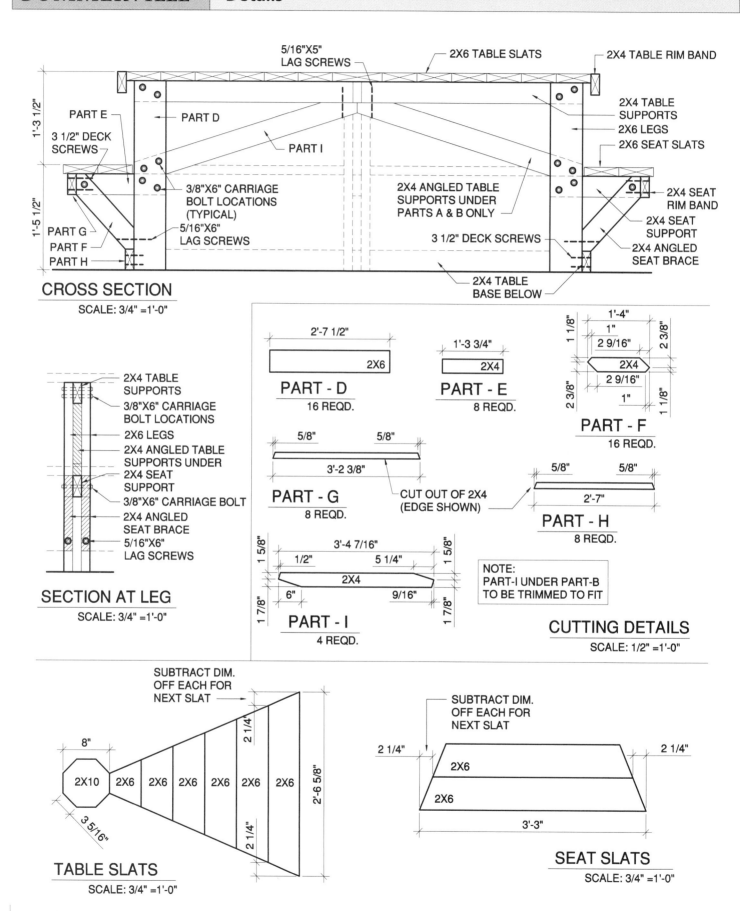

CROSS SECTION
SCALE: 3/4" =1'-0"

5/16"X5" LAG SCREWS
2X6 TABLE SLATS
2X4 TABLE RIM BAND
2X4 TABLE SUPPORTS
2X6 LEGS
2X6 SEAT SLATS
PART E
PART D
PART I
1'-3 1/2"
3 1/2" DECK SCREWS
1'-5 1/2"
PART G
PART F
PART H
3/8"X6" CARRIAGE BOLT LOCATIONS (TYPICAL)
5/16"X6" LAG SCREWS
2X4 ANGLED TABLE SUPPORTS UNDER PARTS A & B ONLY
3 1/2" DECK SCREWS
2X4 SEAT RIM BAND
2X4 SEAT SUPPORT
2X4 ANGLED SEAT BRACE
2X4 TABLE BASE BELOW

SECTION AT LEG
SCALE: 3/4" =1'-0"

2X4 TABLE SUPPORTS
3/8"X6" CARRIAGE BOLT LOCATIONS
2X6 LEGS
2X4 ANGLED TABLE SUPPORTS UNDER
2X4 SEAT SUPPORT
3/8"X6" CARRIAGE BOLT
2X4 ANGLED SEAT BRACE
5/16"X6" LAG SCREWS

2'-7 1/2"
2X6
PART - D
16 REQD.

1'-3 3/4"
2X4
PART - E
8 REQD.

1'-4"
1"
2 9/16"
1 1/8"
2 3/8"
2X4
2 9/16"
2 3/8"
1 1/8"
1"
PART - F
16 REQD.

5/8" 5/8"
3'-2 3/8"
PART - G
8 REQD.
CUT OUT OF 2X4 (EDGE SHOWN)

5/8" 5/8"
2'-7"
PART - H
8 REQD.

1 5/8"
3'-4 7/16"
1 5/8"
1/2"
5 1/4"
2X4
1 7/8"
6"
9/16"
1 7/8"
PART - I
4 REQD.

NOTE:
PART-I UNDER PART-B TO BE TRIMMED TO FIT

CUTTING DETAILS
SCALE: 1/2" =1'-0"

SUBTRACT DIM. OFF EACH FOR NEXT SLAT
8"
2X10
2X6 2X6 2X6 2X6 2X6 2X6
2 1/4"
2 1/4"
2'-6 5/8"
3 5/16"
TABLE SLATS
SCALE: 3/4" =1'-0"

SUBTRACT DIM. OFF EACH FOR NEXT SLAT
2 1/4"
2 1/4"
2X6
2X6
3'-3"
SEAT SLATS
SCALE: 3/4" =1'-0"

PICNIC TABLE

Item	Location	Qty	UM
2x6 - 8' Redwood	Leg/Seat/Top	24	EA
2x4 - 8' Redwood	Support	20	EA
3/8"x6" Carr. Bolt	Leg/Support	60	EA
3/8" Hex Nut	Leg/Support	60	EA
3/8"x3/4" Washer	Leg/Support	60	EA
5/16"x5" Lag Screw	Support	6	EA
5/16"x6" Lag Screw	Support	28	EA
5# 2-1/2" Coated Screws	General	1	EA
5# 3-1/2" Coated Screws	Rim Band	1	EA

THE KIDSRULE

HPM-1711

Wraparound seating on this picnic table makes the most of your building materials and your outdoor living space. Building it yourself will save you some money in the process! The kids will enjoy the table's not-so-big size.

Dimensions for this picnic table are 6' X 4'.

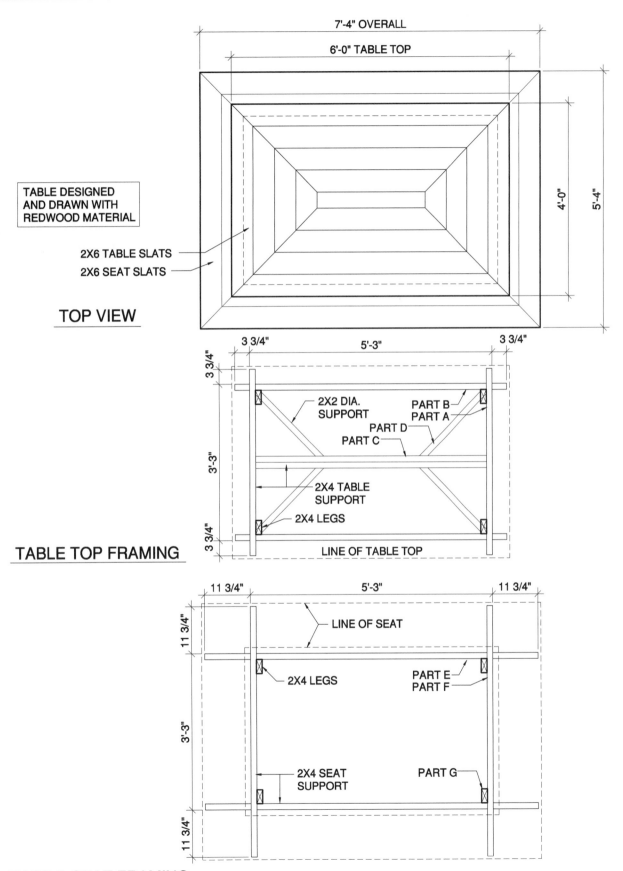

7'-4" OVERALL

6'-0" TABLE TOP

4'-0"

5'-4"

TABLE DESIGNED
AND DRAWN WITH
REDWOOD MATERIAL

2X6 TABLE SLATS

2X6 SEAT SLATS

TOP VIEW

3 3/4"   5'-3"   3 3/4"

3 3/4"

2X2 DIA. SUPPORT

PART B
PART A

PART D
PART C

3'-3"

2X4 TABLE SUPPORT

3 3/4"

2X4 LEGS

LINE OF TABLE TOP

TABLE TOP FRAMING

11 3/4"   5'-3"   11 3/4"

11 3/4"

LINE OF SEAT

2X4 LEGS

PART E
PART F

3'-3"

2X4 SEAT SUPPORT

PART G

11 3/4"

BASE & SEAT FRAMING

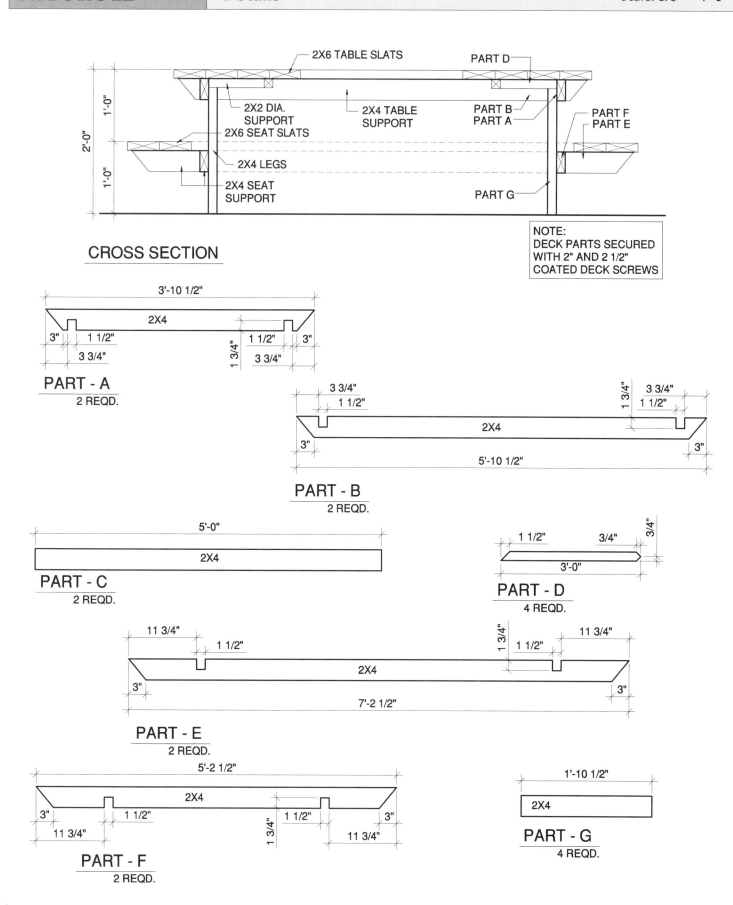

CROSS SECTION

2X6 TABLE SLATS

PART D

2X2 DIA. SUPPORT

2X4 TABLE SUPPORT

2X6 SEAT SLATS

PART B
PART A

PART F
PART E

2X4 LEGS

2X4 SEAT SUPPORT

PART G

NOTE:
DECK PARTS SECURED WITH 2" AND 2 1/2" COATED DECK SCREWS

PART - A
2 REQD.

3'-10 1/2"
2X4
3" 1 1/2" 1 1/2" 3"
3 3/4" 1 3/4" 3 3/4"

PART - B
2 REQD.

3 3/4"
1 1/2"
1 3/4"
3 3/4"
1 1/2"
3"
2X4
3"
5'-10 1/2"

PART - C
2 REQD.

5'-0"
2X4

PART - D
4 REQD.

1 1/2" 3/4" 3/4"
3'-0"

PART - E
2 REQD.

11 3/4"
1 1/2"
1 3/4"
1 1/2"
11 3/4"
3" 2X4 3"
7'-2 1/2"

PART - F
2 REQD.

5'-2 1/2"
2X4
3" 1 1/2" 1 3/4" 1 1/2" 3"
11 3/4" 11 3/4"

PART - G
4 REQD.

1'-10 1/2"
2X4

PICNIC TABLE

Item	Location	Qty	UM
2x6 - 8' Redwood	Seat/Top	18	EA
2x4 - 8' Redwood	Support Part A/B/C/E/F/G	8	EA
2X2 - 8' Redwood	Support Part D	2	EA
5# 2-1/2" Coated Screws	General	1	EA
5# 2" Coated Screws	General	1	EA

THE CEDARVILLE

HPM-1607

Enjoy hours of relaxation outdoors in this lovely gazebo. Its open octagonal design welcomes you from every side. The fully shingled roof provides shade from the sun as well as shelter from the rain.

Dimensions for this gazebo are 8' X 8'.

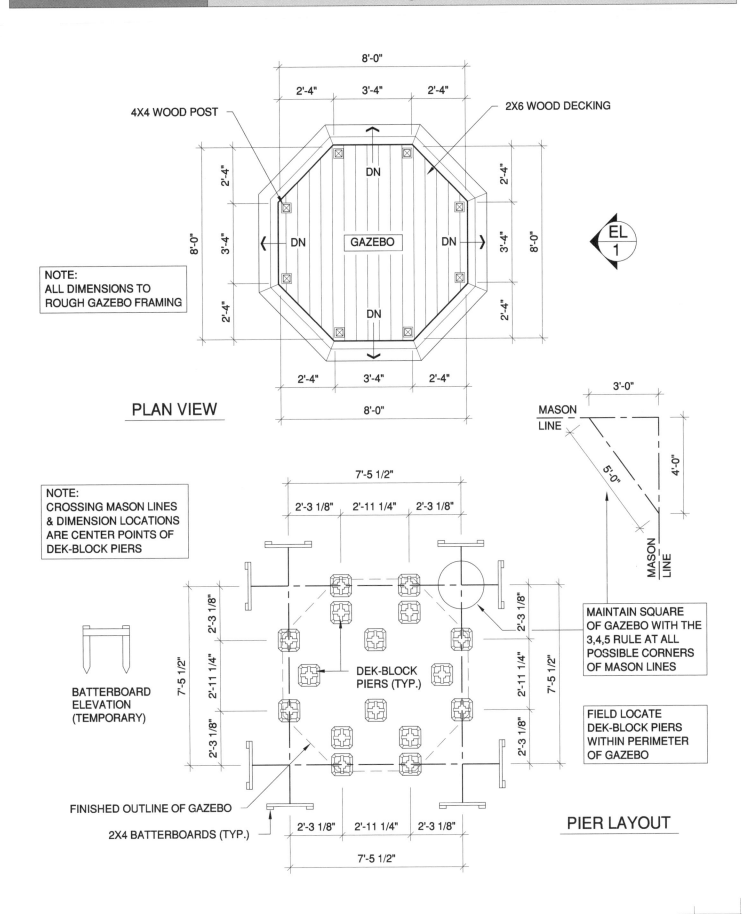

PLAN VIEW

4X4 WOOD POST

2X6 WOOD DECKING

DN

DN   GAZEBO   DN

DN

EL 1

NOTE:
ALL DIMENSIONS TO
ROUGH GAZEBO FRAMING

8'-0"
2'-4"   3'-4"   2'-4"
2'-4"   3'-4"   2'-4"   8'-0"
8'-0"
2'-4"   3'-4"   2'-4"
2'-4"   3'-4"   2'-4"
8'-0"

MASON LINE
3'-0"
5'-0"
4'-0"
MASON LINE

NOTE:
CROSSING MASON LINES
& DIMENSION LOCATIONS
ARE CENTER POINTS OF
DEK-BLOCK PIERS

BATTERBOARD
ELEVATION
(TEMPORARY)

DEK-BLOCK
PIERS (TYP.)

MAINTAIN SQUARE
OF GAZEBO WITH THE
3,4,5 RULE AT ALL
POSSIBLE CORNERS
OF MASON LINES

FIELD LOCATE
DEK-BLOCK PIERS
WITHIN PERIMETER
OF GAZEBO

FINISHED OUTLINE OF GAZEBO

2X4 BATTERBOARDS (TYP.)

7'-5 1/2"
2'-3 1/8"   2'-11 1/4"   2'-3 1/8"
2'-3 1/8"   2'-11 1/4"   2'-3 1/8"   7'-5 1/2"
7'-5 1/2"
2'-3 1/8"   2'-11 1/4"   2'-3 1/8"
2'-3 1/8"   2'-11 1/4"   2'-3 1/8"
7'-5 1/2"

PIER LAYOUT

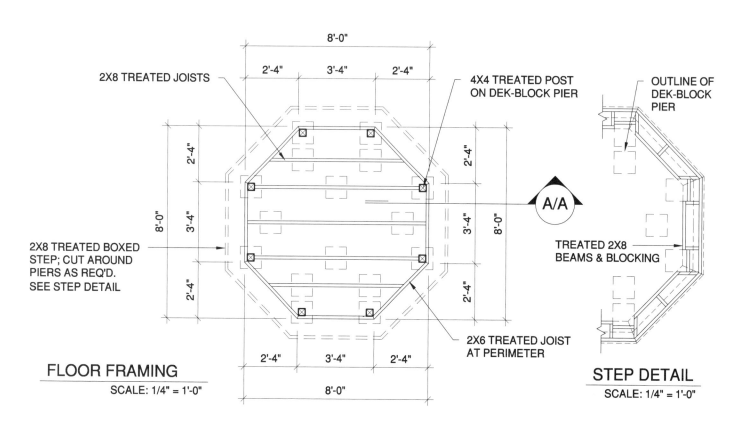

2X8 TREATED JOISTS

4X4 TREATED POST ON DEK-BLOCK PIER

OUTLINE OF DEK-BLOCK PIER

2X8 TREATED BOXED STEP; CUT AROUND PIERS AS REQ'D. SEE STEP DETAIL

TREATED 2X8 BEAMS & BLOCKING

A/A

2X6 TREATED JOIST AT PERIMETER

8'-0"
2'-4"   3'-4"   2'-4"

FLOOR FRAMING
SCALE: 1/4" = 1'-0"

STEP DETAIL
SCALE: 1/4" = 1'-0"

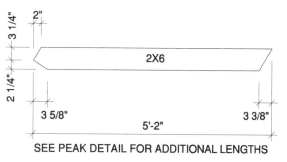

2X6

2"   3 1/4"   2 1/4"

3 5/8"   3 3/8"

5'-2"

SEE PEAK DETAIL FOR ADDITIONAL LENGTHS

2X6 RIDGE RAFTER "A"
SCALE: 1/2" = 1'-0"

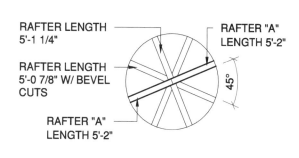

RAFTER LENGTH 5'-1 1/4"

RAFTER "A" LENGTH 5'-2"

RAFTER LENGTH 5'-0 7/8" W/ BEVEL CUTS

RAFTER "A" LENGTH 5'-2"

45°

PEAK DETAIL "B"
SCALE: 1/2" = 1'-0"

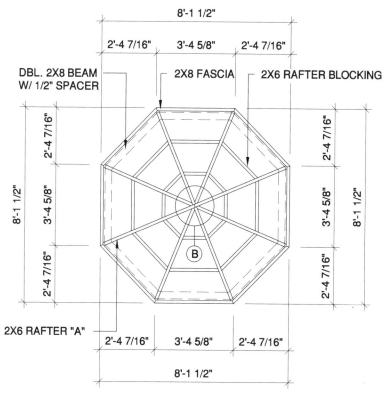

8'-1 1/2"
2'-4 7/16"   3'-4 5/8"   2'-4 7/16"

DBL. 2X8 BEAM W/ 1/2" SPACER

2X8 FASCIA

2X6 RAFTER BLOCKING

2X6 RAFTER "A"

B

2'-4 7/16"   3'-4 5/8"   2'-4 7/16"
8'-1 1/2"

ROOF FRAMING
SCALE: 1/4" = 1'-0"

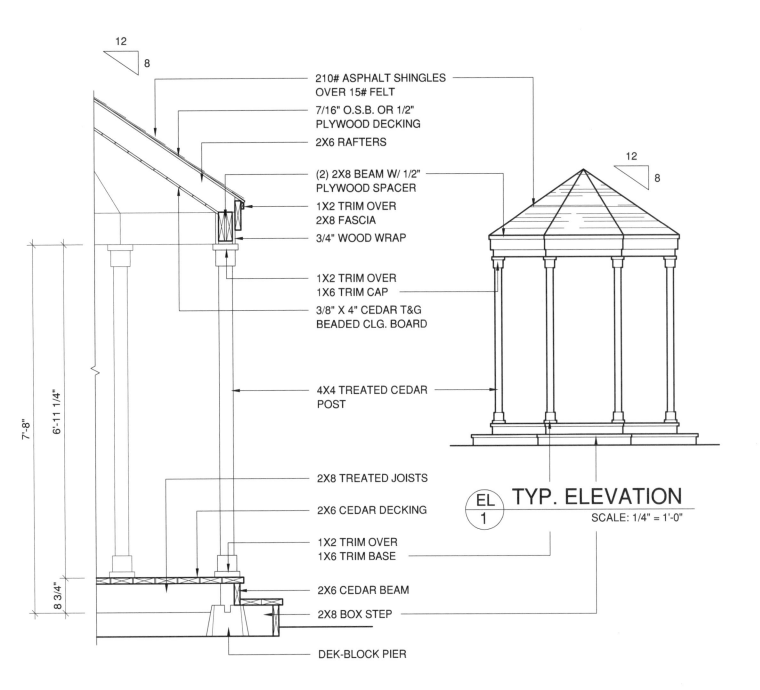

12 / 8

210# ASPHALT SHINGLES OVER 15# FELT

7/16" O.S.B. OR 1/2" PLYWOOD DECKING

2X6 RAFTERS

(2) 2X8 BEAM W/ 1/2" PLYWOOD SPACER

1X2 TRIM OVER 2X8 FASCIA

3/4" WOOD WRAP

1X2 TRIM OVER 1X6 TRIM CAP

3/8" X 4" CEDAR T&G BEADED CLG. BOARD

4X4 TREATED CEDAR POST

2X8 TREATED JOISTS

2X6 CEDAR DECKING

1X2 TRIM OVER 1X6 TRIM BASE

2X6 CEDAR BEAM

2X8 BOX STEP

DEK-BLOCK PIER

7'-8"

6'-11 1/4"

8 3/4"

SECTION A-A
SCALE: 1/2" = 1'-0"

12 / 8

EL / 1   ## TYP. ELEVATION
SCALE: 1/4" = 1'-0"

GAZEBO FOUNDATION

Item	Location	Qty	UM
Dek-Block Pier	Pier	16	EA
2x4 - 10' Std. & Btr.	Pier	5	EA

GAZEBO DECK FRAMING

Item	Location	Qty	UM
4x4 - 8' Cedar	Post	8	EA
2x8 - 8' Treated	Joist	5	EA
2x8 - 8' Treated	Box Step	5	EA
2x6 - 8' Cedar	Perimeter Joist	4	EA
2x6 - 8' Cedar	Deck/Tread	27	EA
2x8 - 10' Cedar	Box Step Perimeter	4	EA
5# 16d Galv. Nails	General Framing	4	EA
5# 8d Ctd. Box Nails	General Framing	1	EA
1# 2-1/2" Ctd. Screws	Decking	1	EA
Construction Adhesive	Decking	2	EA

GAZEBO ROOF/CEILING FRAMING

Item	Location	Qty	UM
2x8 - 8' Treated	Beam	8	EA
1/2" CDX - 5-Ply Plywood	Beam Spacer	1	EA
2x8 - 12' #2 & Btr.	Rafter	4	EA
2x8 - 12' #2 & Btr.	Rafter Blocking	3	EA
7/16" O.S.B. (Ply.)	Roof Decking	4	EA
15-lb. Asphalt Roofing Felt	Roof	1	RL
3 - Tab Shingles 20 Yr.	Roof	5	BN
5# 8d Ctd. Box Nails	General Framing	4	EA
5# 10d Bright Box Nails	General Framing	2	EA
5# 16d Galv. Nails	General Framing	2	EA
5# 6d Galv. Box Nails	General Framing	3	EA
5# 1/2" Roofing Nails	Roofing Felt	1	EA
5# 1-1/4" Roofing Nails	Shingle	2	EA
5# 6d Galv. Finish Nails	Ceiling	5	EA

GAZEBO FINISH TRIM

Item	Location	Qty	UM
2x8 - 8' Cedar	Fascia	4	EA
1x2 - 8' Cedar	Fascia/Post Trim	9	EA
1x6 - 8' Cedar	Post Trim	4	EA
3/4" Cedar Plywood	Beam Wrap	2	EA
3/8"x4" Cedar Beaded Board	Ceiling	71	SF

THE POTTERSVILLE

HPM-1605

Enjoy hot days out of the sun and terrific evenings shielded from pesky insects in the shelter of this screened gazebo. The shingled roof allows you to enjoy it even under a gentle rain. A handsome railing wraps along the bottom of its octagonal structure, while high arches expand the views above. Inside is plenty of space for family dining, board games and relaxation.

Dimensions for this screened gazebo are 12' X 12'.

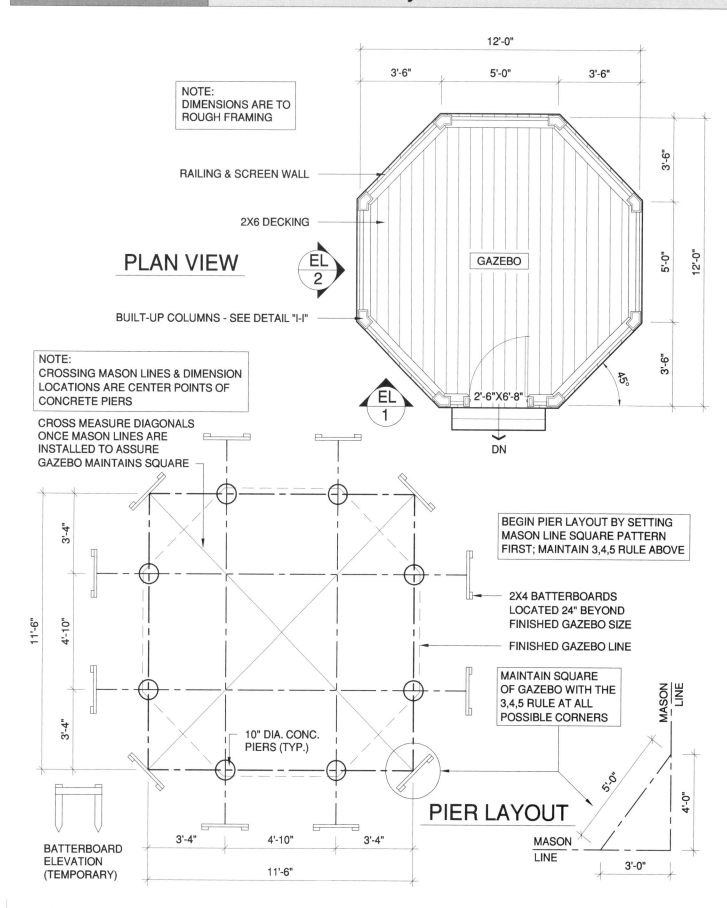

NOTE:
DIMENSIONS ARE TO
ROUGH FRAMING

RAILING & SCREEN WALL

2X6 DECKING

PLAN VIEW

BUILT-UP COLUMNS - SEE DETAIL "I-I"

NOTE:
CROSSING MASON LINES & DIMENSION
LOCATIONS ARE CENTER POINTS OF
CONCRETE PIERS

CROSS MEASURE DIAGONALS
ONCE MASON LINES ARE
INSTALLED TO ASSURE
GAZEBO MAINTAINS SQUARE

GAZEBO

2'-6"X6'-8"

DN

EL 2

EL 1

12'-0"
3'-6"   5'-0"   3'-6"
3'-6"   5'-0"   3'-6"   12'-0"
45°

BEGIN PIER LAYOUT BY SETTING
MASON LINE SQUARE PATTERN
FIRST; MAINTAIN 3,4,5 RULE ABOVE

2X4 BATTERBOARDS
LOCATED 24" BEYOND
FINISHED GAZEBO SIZE

FINISHED GAZEBO LINE

MAINTAIN SQUARE
OF GAZEBO WITH THE
3,4,5 RULE AT ALL
POSSIBLE CORNERS

10" DIA. CONC.
PIERS (TYP.)

PIER LAYOUT

3'-4"
4'-10"
11'-6"
3'-4"

3'-4"   4'-10"   3'-4"
11'-6"

MASON LINE
MASON LINE
5'-0"
4'-0"
3'-0"

BATTERBOARD
ELEVATION
(TEMPORARY)

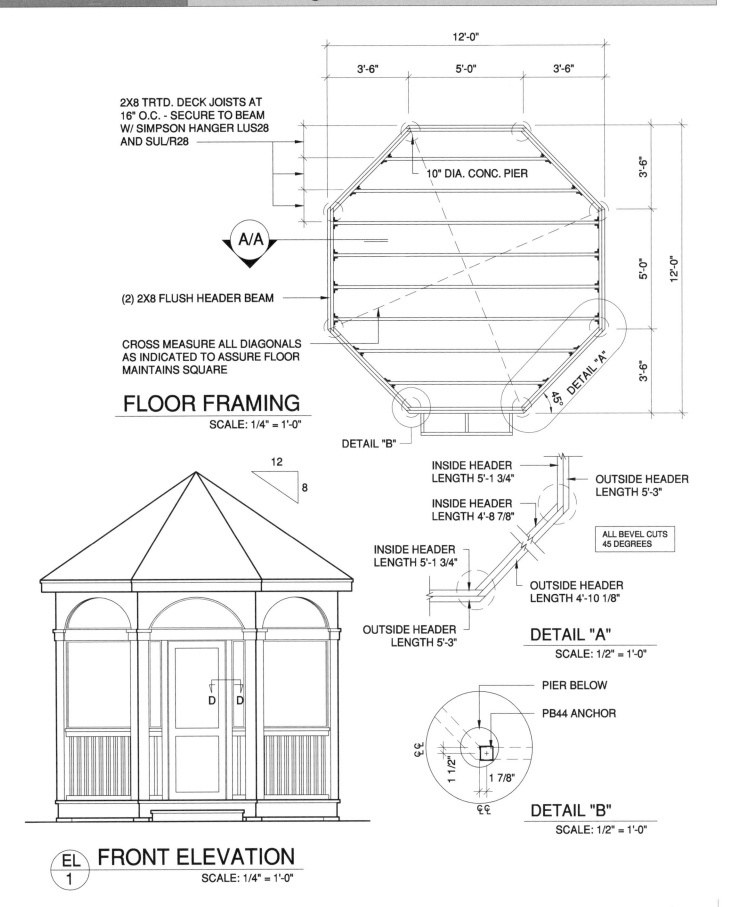

12'-0"

3'-6" 5'-0" 3'-6"

2X8 TRTD. DECK JOISTS AT
16" O.C. - SECURE TO BEAM
W/ SIMPSON HANGER LUS28
AND SUL/R28

10" DIA. CONC. PIER

A/A

3'-6"

5'-0" 12'-0"

(2) 2X8 FLUSH HEADER BEAM

CROSS MEASURE ALL DIAGONALS
AS INDICATED TO ASSURE FLOOR
MAINTAINS SQUARE

3'-6"

45° DETAIL "A"

FLOOR FRAMING
SCALE: 1/4" = 1'-0"

DETAIL "B"

12

8

INSIDE HEADER
LENGTH 5'-1 3/4"

OUTSIDE HEADER
LENGTH 5'-3"

INSIDE HEADER
LENGTH 4'-8 7/8"

INSIDE HEADER
LENGTH 5'-1 3/4"

ALL BEVEL CUTS
45 DEGREES

OUTSIDE HEADER
LENGTH 4'-10 1/8"

OUTSIDE HEADER
LENGTH 5'-3"

DETAIL "A"
SCALE: 1/2" = 1'-0"

D D

PIER BELOW

PB44 ANCHOR

1 1/2" 1 7/8"

DETAIL "B"
SCALE: 1/2" = 1'-0"

EL
1
FRONT ELEVATION
SCALE: 1/4" = 1'-0"

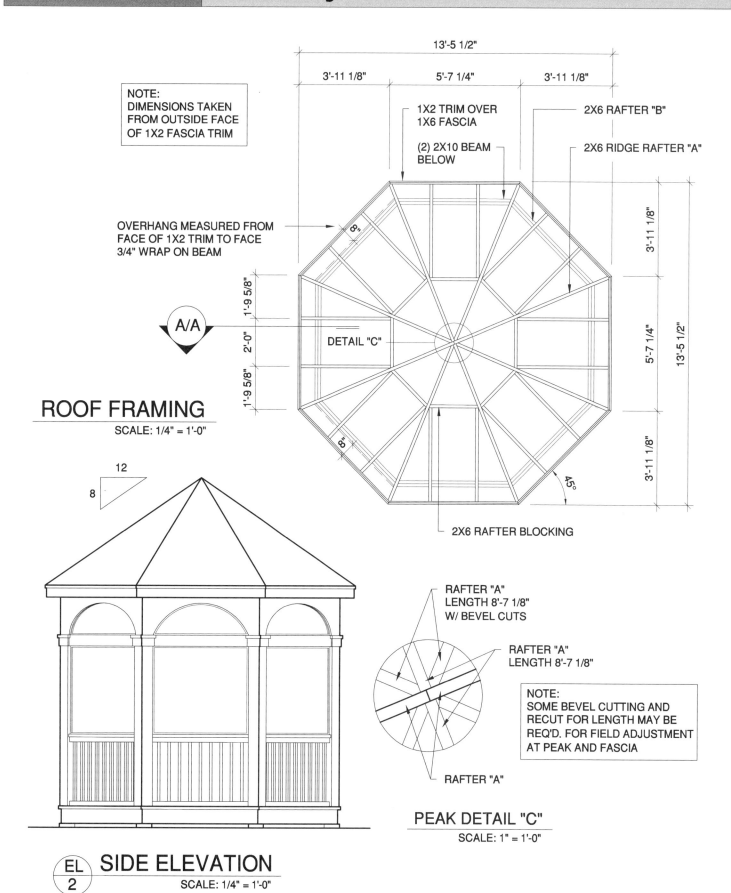

NOTE:
DIMENSIONS TAKEN FROM OUTSIDE FACE OF 1X2 FASCIA TRIM

OVERHANG MEASURED FROM FACE OF 1X2 TRIM TO FACE 3/4" WRAP ON BEAM

A/A

ROOF FRAMING
SCALE: 1/4" = 1'-0"

13'-5 1/2"

3'-11 1/8" 5'-7 1/4" 3'-11 1/8"

1X2 TRIM OVER 1X6 FASCIA

(2) 2X10 BEAM BELOW

2X6 RAFTER "B"

2X6 RIDGE RAFTER "A"

3'-11 1/8"

5'-7 1/4"

13'-5 1/2"

3'-11 1/8"

8"

8"

45°

DETAIL "C"

2X6 RAFTER BLOCKING

12
8

SIDE ELEVATION
EL 2
SCALE: 1/4" = 1'-0"

RAFTER "A" LENGTH 8'-7 1/8" W/ BEVEL CUTS

RAFTER "A" LENGTH 8'-7 1/8"

NOTE:
SOME BEVEL CUTTING AND RECUT FOR LENGTH MAY BE REQ'D. FOR FIELD ADJUSTMENT AT PEAK AND FASCIA

RAFTER "A"

PEAK DETAIL "C"
SCALE: 1" = 1'-0"

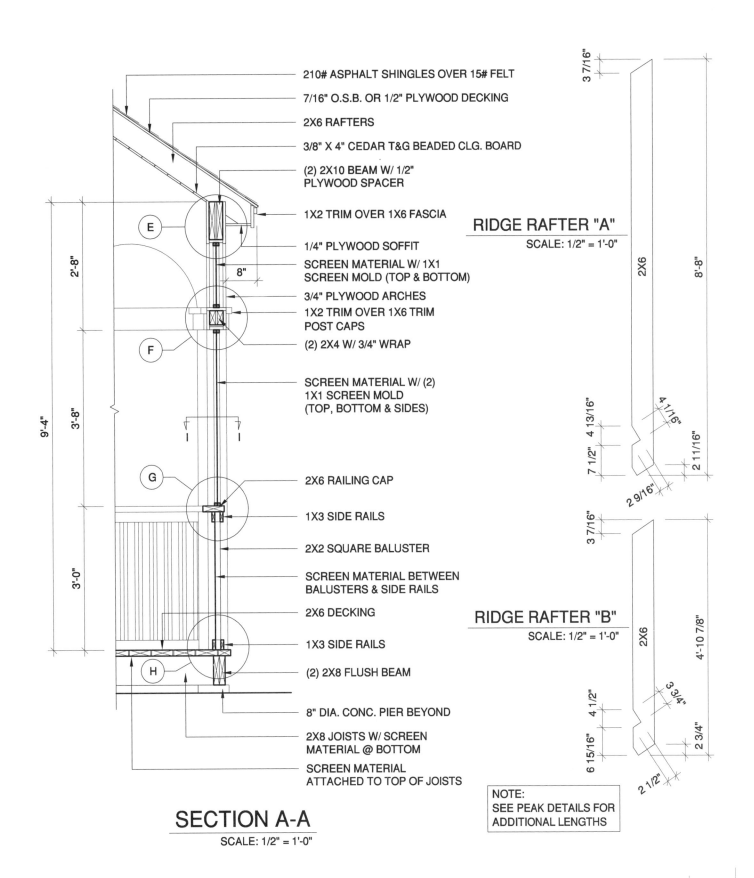

210# ASPHALT SHINGLES OVER 15# FELT

7/16" O.S.B. OR 1/2" PLYWOOD DECKING

2X6 RAFTERS

3/8" X 4" CEDAR T&G BEADED CLG. BOARD

(2) 2X10 BEAM W/ 1/2"
PLYWOOD SPACER

1X2 TRIM OVER 1X6 FASCIA

1/4" PLYWOOD SOFFIT

SCREEN MATERIAL W/ 1X1
SCREEN MOLD (TOP & BOTTOM)

3/4" PLYWOOD ARCHES

1X2 TRIM OVER 1X6 TRIM
POST CAPS

(2) 2X4 W/ 3/4" WRAP

SCREEN MATERIAL W/ (2)
1X1 SCREEN MOLD
(TOP, BOTTOM & SIDES)

2X6 RAILING CAP

1X3 SIDE RAILS

2X2 SQUARE BALUSTER

SCREEN MATERIAL BETWEEN
BALUSTERS & SIDE RAILS

2X6 DECKING

1X3 SIDE RAILS

(2) 2X8 FLUSH BEAM

8" DIA. CONC. PIER BEYOND

2X8 JOISTS W/ SCREEN
MATERIAL @ BOTTOM

SCREEN MATERIAL
ATTACHED TO TOP OF JOISTS

SECTION A-A
SCALE: 1/2" = 1'-0"

RIDGE RAFTER "A"
SCALE: 1/2" = 1'-0"

RIDGE RAFTER "B"
SCALE: 1/2" = 1'-0"

NOTE:
SEE PEAK DETAILS FOR
ADDITIONAL LENGTHS

RAILING BELOW

SCREEN DOOR

1/2" X 1" DOOR STOP

VERTICAL 2X4
W/ 3/4" WRAP

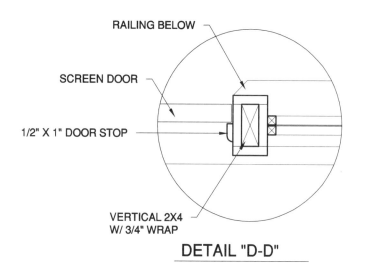

DETAIL "D-D"

SCREEN MATERIAL

(2) 1X1 SCREEN
MOLD

SCREEN MATERIAL
(SECURED BETWEEN
1X3 SIDE RAIL & 2X2
BALUSTERS)

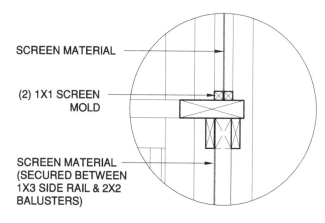

DETAIL "G"

(2) 1X1 SCREEN
MOLD

SCREEN MATERIAL

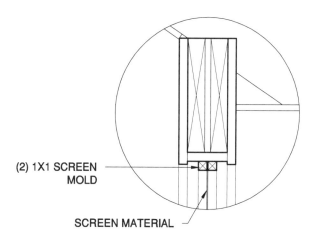

DETAIL "E"

SCREEN MATERIAL
(SECURED BETWEEN
1X3 SIDE RAIL & 2X2
BALUSTERS)

SOLID BLOCKING
BETWEEN RAILS

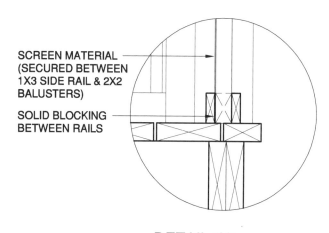

DETAIL "H"

SCREEN MATERIAL

(2) 1X1 SCREEN
MOLD

1/2" WOOD SHIM

SCREEN MATERIAL

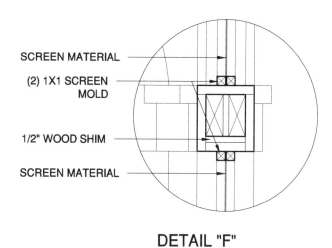

DETAIL "F"

3/4" WRAP

1X1 SCREEN MOLD

SCREEN MATERIAL

RAILING BELOW

2X4 CONSTRUCTION
AT ALL CORNERS

2X2 NAILER

4 1/2"

3/4"

4 1/2"

3/4"

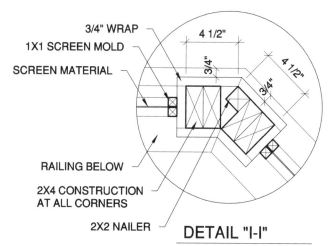

DETAIL "I-I"

FOUNDATION

Item	Location	Qty	UM
60# Concrete Mix	Pier	40	BG
10"x48" Fiber Tube	Pier	8	EA
2x4 - 10' Std. & Btr.	Batterboard	8	EA
Post Base (PB44)	Pier	8	EA
Crushed Stone	Pier	16	BG
5# 16d Galvanized Nails	General Framing	1	EA
5# 8d Coated Box Nails	General Framing	1	EA

FRAMING

Item	Location	Qty	UM
2x8 - 12' Treated	Beam	8	EA
2x8 - 8' Treated	Joist	2	EA
2x8 - 10' Treated	Joist	2	EA
2x8 - 12' Treated	Joist	4	EA
2x6 - 12' Treated	Step	1	EA
2x8 Joist Hanger (LUS28)	Joist	8	EA
2x8 Joist Hanger (Angled) (SUR26)	Joist	4	EA
2x8 Joist Hanger (Angled) (SUL26)	Joist	4	EA
1# 8d Hanger Nails	Connector	3	EA
5# 16d Galv. Nails	General Framing	3	EA
5# 8d Ctd. Box Nails	General Framing	1	EA

WALL FRAMING

Item	Location	Qty	UM
2x4 - 10' Std. & Btr. Doug. Fir	Wall/Door Corner	36	EA
2x2 - 10' #2 & Btr. Doug. Fir	Wall Corner Nailer	8	EA
2x4 - 10' Std. & Btr. Doug. Fir	Wall Header	8	EA
1/2" - CDX - 5 Ply Plywood	Header/Shim	1	EA
5# 16d Galv. Nails	General Framing	2	EA
5# 8d Ctd. Box Nails	General Framing	2	EA

ROOF FRAMING

Item	Location	Qty	UM
2x10 - 12' #2 & Btr. Doug. Fir	Beam	8	EA
1/2" - CDX - 5 Ply Plywood	Beam	2	EA
2x6 -10' #2 & Btr. Doug. Fir	Rafter/Blocking	19	EA
7/16" - 4x8 OSB	Roof Decking	8	EA
15-lb. Roofing Felt	Roof	1	RL
Classic 3 - Tab 20 Year Shingle	Roof	10	BN
5# 16d Galv. Nails	General Framing	1	EA
5# 8d Zinc Coated Box Nails	General Framing	2	EA
5# 10d Bright Box Nails	General Framing	2	EA
5# 6d Galvanized Box Nails	General Framing	1	EA
5# 6d Galvanized Finish Nails	Soffit/Ceiling	1	EA
5# 1/2" Roofing Nails	Roofing Felt	1	EA
5# 1-1/4" Roofing Nails	Shingle	2	EA

FINISH/RAILING

Item	Location	Qty	UM
2x6 - 12' Treated	Decking/Tread	22	EA
2x6 - 16' Treated	Decking/Tread	2	EA
2x6 - 10' Treated	Railing Cap	4	EA
1x3 - 10' Treated	Siderail	16	EA
2"x2" - 3' Square Baluster	Baluster	76	EA
2x3 - 10' Treated	Blstr. Blocking	8	EA
1x1 - 4' Square Stock	Screen Mold	34	EA
1x1 - 6' Square Stock	Screen Mold	68	EA
Fiberglass Screen (48"x25')	Screen	8	RL
30"x80" Screen Dr. w/Hrdwr. Kit	Door	1	EA
1/2"x1" Door Stop	Door	20	LF
1/4" Plywood (Sanded)	Soffit	1	EA
1x2 - 8' Std. & Btr.	Top Post Trim	12	EA
1x6 - 8' Std. & Btr.	Top Post Trim	12	EA
3/8"x4" Cedar Beaded Board	Ceiling	428	SF
3/4" - 4x8 Sq. Edge Plywood	Arch Panel	9	EA
1x4 - 8' Std. & Btr.	Door/Post Wrap	24	EA
1x6 - 8' Std. & Btr.	Post Wrap	32	EA
1x6 - 10' Std. & Btr.	Header Wrap	16	EA
1# 2-1/2" Ctd. Screws	Decking/Railing	10	EA
5# 16d Galv. Nails	General Framing	2	EA
5# 8d Ctd. Box Nails	General Framing	1	EA
5# 4d Galvanized Finish Nails	Finish Framing	1	EA
5# 6d Galvanized Finish Nails	Finish Framing	3	EA
5# 8d Galvanized Finish Nails	Finish Framing	3	EA
Construction Adhesive	General Framing	2	TB

THE TRESTLE

HPM-1606

This gazebo/deck combination makes enjoying the outdoors the life of luxury. The spacious 14'x10' deck is the place for fun in the sun, while the gazebo provides a shaded shelter for those who prefer a cooler atmosphere. Make the most of those irresistible summer evenings in the gazebo's screened haven.

Dimensions for this gazebo/deck are 26' X 13'6".

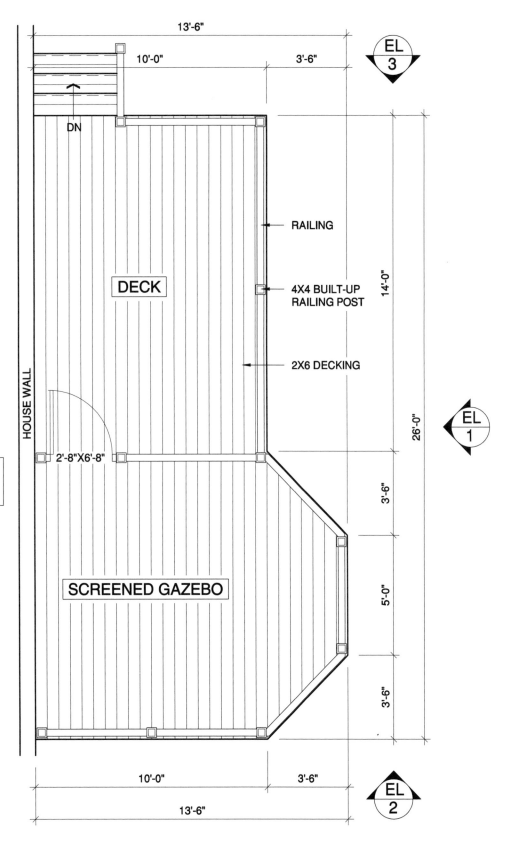

13'-6"

10'-0"

3'-6"

EL 3

DN

RAILING

DECK

4X4 BUILT-UP
RAILING POST

14'-0"

2X6 DECKING

EL 1

26'-0"

STAIR QUANTITY
BASED ON SITE
CONDITIONS

HOUSE WALL

2'-8"X6'-8"

3'-6"

NOTE:
DIMENSIONS ARE
TO ROUGH FRAMING

SCREENED GAZEBO

5'-0"

3'-6"

10'-0"

3'-6"

EL 2

13'-6"

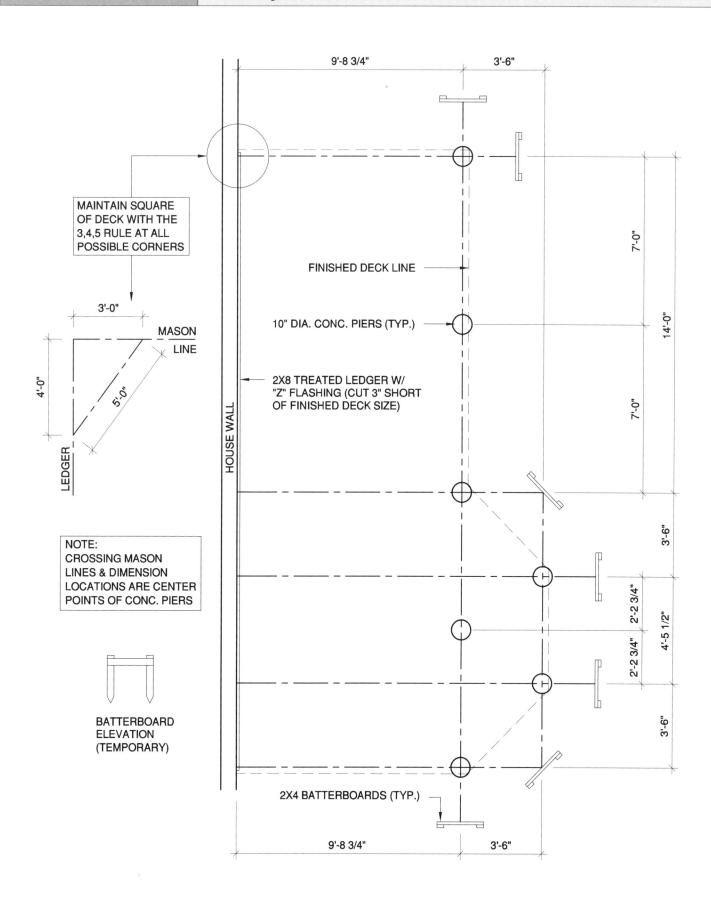

MAINTAIN SQUARE
OF DECK WITH THE
3,4,5 RULE AT ALL
POSSIBLE CORNERS

MASON
LINE

LEDGER

NOTE:
CROSSING MASON
LINES & DIMENSION
LOCATIONS ARE CENTER
POINTS OF CONC. PIERS

BATTERBOARD
ELEVATION
(TEMPORARY)

FINISHED DECK LINE

10" DIA. CONC. PIERS (TYP.)

2X8 TREATED LEDGER W/
"Z" FLASHING (CUT 3" SHORT
OF FINISHED DECK SIZE)

HOUSE WALL

2X4 BATTERBOARDS (TYP.)

9'-8 3/4"   3'-6"

7'-0"

14'-0"

7'-0"

3'-6"

2'-2 3/4"

4'-5 1/2"

2'-2 3/4"

3'-6"

3'-0"

4'-0"

5'-0"

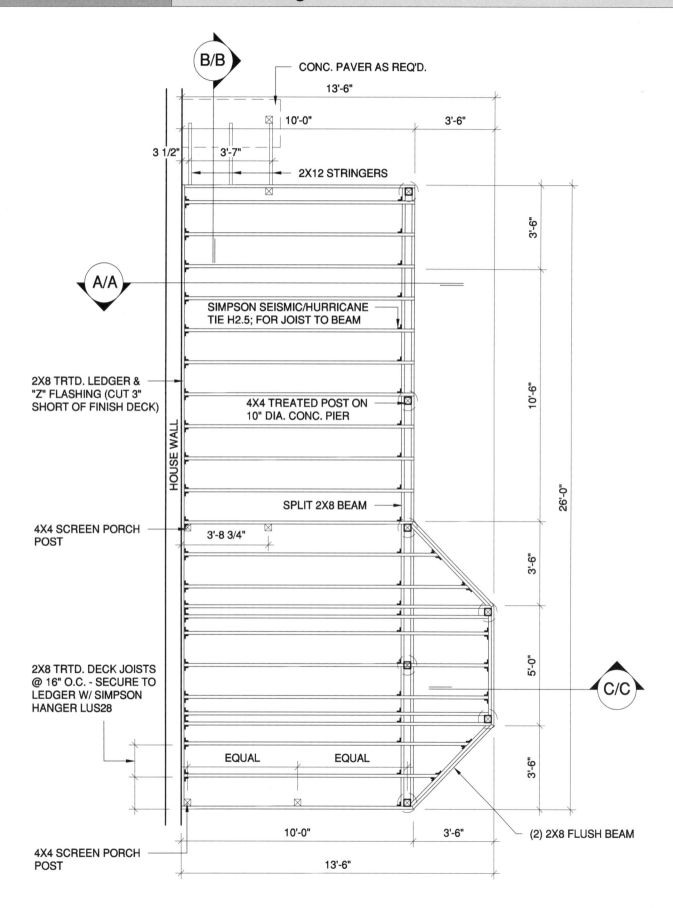

B/B

CONC. PAVER AS REQ'D.

13'-6"

10'-0"   3'-6"

3 1/2"

3'-7"

2X12 STRINGERS

3'-6"

A/A

SIMPSON SEISMIC/HURRICANE
TIE H2.5; FOR JOIST TO BEAM

2X8 TRTD. LEDGER &
"Z" FLASHING (CUT 3"
SHORT OF FINISH DECK)

4X4 TREATED POST ON
10" DIA. CONC. PIER

10'-6"

HOUSE WALL

SPLIT 2X8 BEAM

26'-0"

4X4 SCREEN PORCH
POST

3'-8 3/4"

3'-6"

2X8 TRTD. DECK JOISTS
@ 16" O.C. - SECURE TO
LEDGER W/ SIMPSON
HANGER LUS28

C/C

5'-0"

EQUAL   EQUAL

3'-6"

10'-0"   3'-6"

(2) 2X8 FLUSH BEAM

4X4 SCREEN PORCH
POST

13'-6"

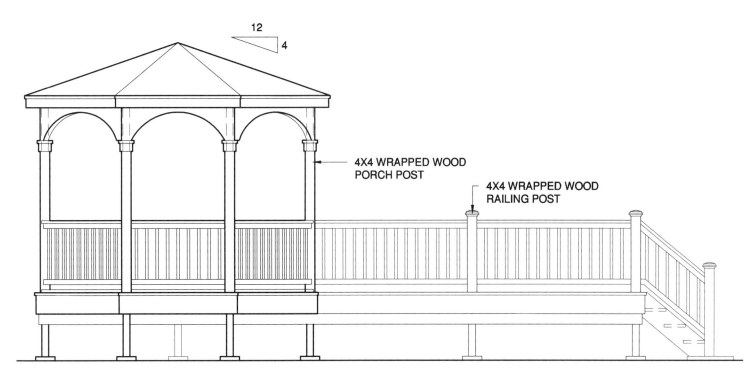

12
4

4X4 WRAPPED WOOD
PORCH POST

4X4 WRAPPED WOOD
RAILING POST

EL
1

FRONT ELEVATION

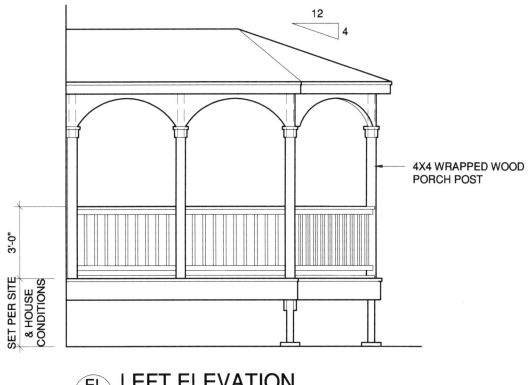

12
4

4X4 WRAPPED WOOD
PORCH POST

3'-0"

SET PER SITE
& HOUSE
CONDITIONS

EL
2

LEFT ELEVATION

RIGHT ELEVATION

SCALE: 1/4" = 1'-0"

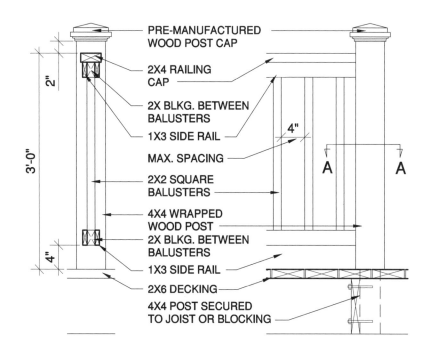

PRE-MANUFACTURED WOOD POST CAP

2X4 RAILING CAP

2X BLKG. BETWEEN BALUSTERS

1X3 SIDE RAIL

MAX. SPACING

2X2 SQUARE BALUSTERS

4X4 WRAPPED WOOD POST

2X BLKG. BETWEEN BALUSTERS

1X3 SIDE RAIL

2X6 DECKING

4X4 POST SECURED TO JOIST OR BLOCKING

2"

3'-0"

4"

4"

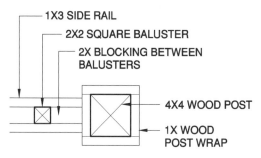

1X3 SIDE RAIL

2X2 SQUARE BALUSTER

2X BLOCKING BETWEEN BALUSTERS

4X4 WOOD POST

1X WOOD POST WRAP

DETAIL A-A

SCALE: 1 1/2" = 1'-0"

RAILING DETAIL

SCALE: 3/4" = 1'-0"

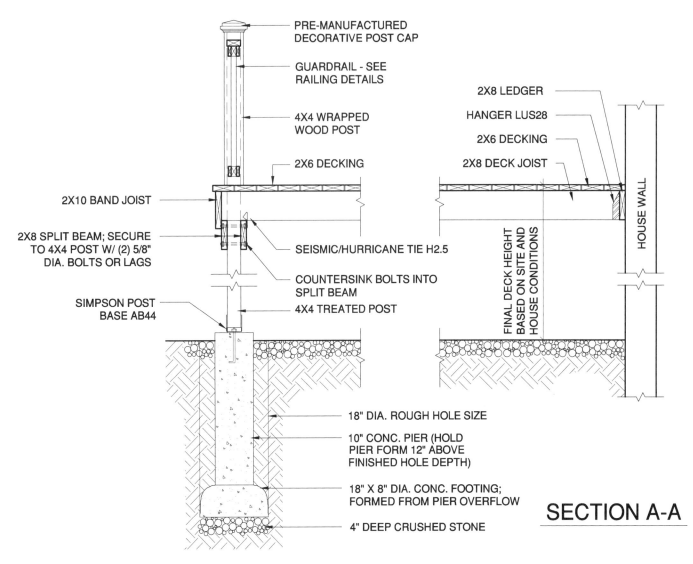

PRE-MANUFACTURED
DECORATIVE POST CAP

GUARDRAIL - SEE
RAILING DETAILS

4X4 WRAPPED
WOOD POST

2X6 DECKING

2X10 BAND JOIST

2X8 SPLIT BEAM; SECURE
TO 4X4 POST W/ (2) 5/8"
DIA. BOLTS OR LAGS

SEISMIC/HURRICANE TIE H2.5

COUNTERSINK BOLTS INTO
SPLIT BEAM

SIMPSON POST
BASE AB44

4X4 TREATED POST

2X8 LEDGER

HANGER LUS28

2X6 DECKING

2X8 DECK JOIST

HOUSE WALL

FINAL DECK HEIGHT
BASED ON SITE AND
HOUSE CONDITIONS

18" DIA. ROUGH HOLE SIZE

10" CONC. PIER (HOLD
PIER FORM 12" ABOVE
FINISHED HOLE DEPTH)

18" X 8" DIA. CONC. FOOTING;
FORMED FROM PIER OVERFLOW

4" DEEP CRUSHED STONE

SECTION A-A

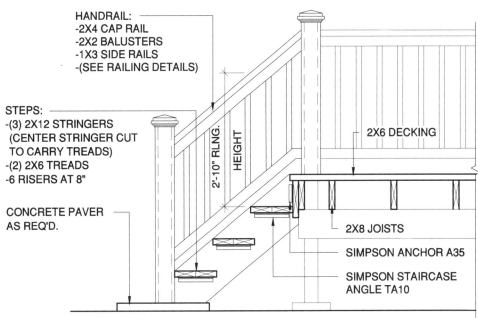

HANDRAIL:
-2X4 CAP RAIL
-2X2 BALUSTERS
-1X3 SIDE RAILS
-(SEE RAILING DETAILS)

STEPS:
-(3) 2X12 STRINGERS
 (CENTER STRINGER CUT
 TO CARRY TREADS)
-(2) 2X6 TREADS
-6 RISERS AT 8"

CONCRETE PAVER
AS REQ'D.

2'-10" RLNG.
HEIGHT

2X6 DECKING

2X8 JOISTS

SIMPSON ANCHOR A35

SIMPSON STAIRCASE
ANGLE TA10

SECTION B-B

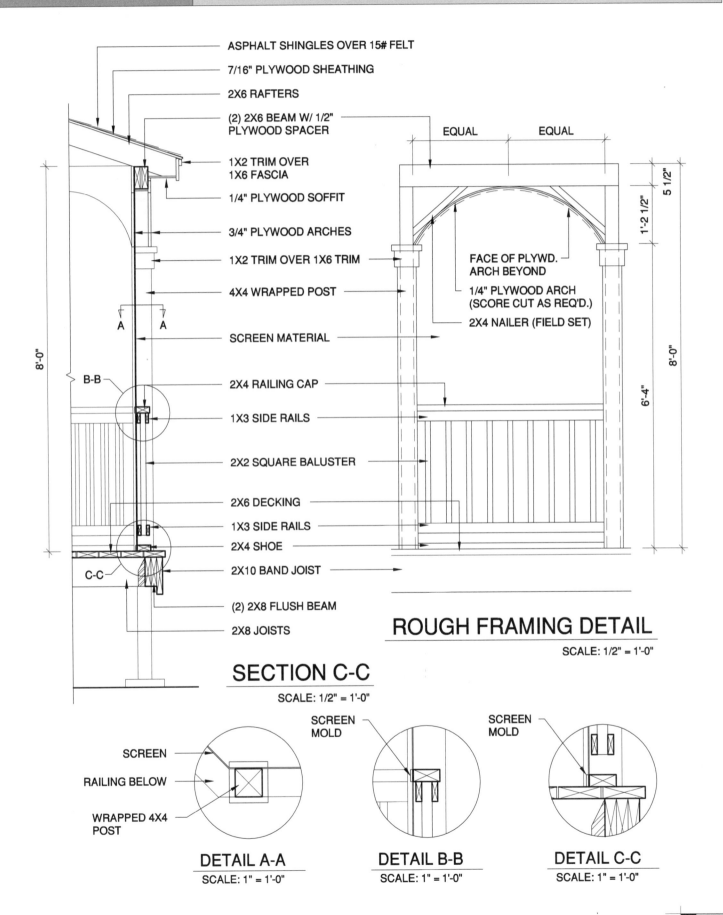

ASPHALT SHINGLES OVER 15# FELT

7/16" PLYWOOD SHEATHING

2X6 RAFTERS

(2) 2X6 BEAM W/ 1/2" PLYWOOD SPACER

1X2 TRIM OVER 1X6 FASCIA

1/4" PLYWOOD SOFFIT

3/4" PLYWOOD ARCHES

1X2 TRIM OVER 1X6 TRIM

4X4 WRAPPED POST

SCREEN MATERIAL

2X4 RAILING CAP

1X3 SIDE RAILS

2X2 SQUARE BALUSTER

2X6 DECKING

1X3 SIDE RAILS

2X4 SHOE

2X10 BAND JOIST

(2) 2X8 FLUSH BEAM

2X8 JOISTS

8'-0"

A A

B-B

C-C

SECTION C-C
SCALE: 1/2" = 1'-0"

EQUAL EQUAL

5 1/2"

1'-2 1/2"

FACE OF PLYWD. ARCH BEYOND

1/4" PLYWOOD ARCH (SCORE CUT AS REQ'D.)

2X4 NAILER (FIELD SET)

8'-0"

6'-4"

ROUGH FRAMING DETAIL
SCALE: 1/2" = 1'-0"

SCREEN

RAILING BELOW

WRAPPED 4X4 POST

DETAIL A-A
SCALE: 1" = 1'-0"

SCREEN MOLD

DETAIL B-B
SCALE: 1" = 1'-0"

SCREEN MOLD

DETAIL C-C
SCALE: 1" = 1'-0"

FOUNDATION

Item	Location	Qty	UM
60# Concrete Mix	Pier	35	BG
10"x48" Fiber Tube	Pier	7	EA
2x4 - 10' Std. & Btr.	Batterboard	5	EA
1/2"x6" Anchor Bolt/Nut/Washer	Pier	7	EA
Post Base (ABA44)	Pier	7	EA
Crushed Gravel	Pier	14	BG
2x8 - 14' Treated	Ledger	2	EA
1x5 - 10' Zee Bar	Ledger	3	EA
3/8"x4" Lag Screws	Ledger	36	EA
3/8"x1-1/2" Washer	Ledger	36	EA
5# 16d Galvanized Nails	General Framing	1	EA
5# 8d Coated Box Nails	General Framing	1	EA
10 oz. - Paintable Caulk	Ledger/Bolt	3	TB

FRAMING

Item	Location	Qty	UM
2x8 - 10' Treated	Flush Beam	3	EA
2x8 - 14' Treated	Split Beam	4	EA
2x8 - 10' Treated	Joist/Blocking	14	EA
2x8 - 14' Treated	Joist/Blocking	12	EA
2x10 - 8' Treated	Band Joist	3	EA
2x10 - 10' Treated	Band Joist	3	EA
4x4 - 14' Treated	Post	4	EA
4x4 - 16' Treated	Post	1	EA
2x8 Joist Hanger (LUS28)	Ledger/Beam	26	EA
2x8 Joist Hanger (SUL26)	Beam	2	EA
2x8 Joist Hanger (SUR26)	Beam	2	EA
Hurricane Tie (H2.5)	Joist/Beam	24	EA
Framing Anchor (A34)	Ledger End Jst./Bm.	4	EA
3/8"x4" Lag Screws	Flush Beam	4	EA
3/8"x1-1/2" Washer	Flush Beam	4	EA
5/8"x7" Lag Bolt	Split Beam	10	EA
5/8"x1-1/2" Washer	Split Beam	10	EA
1# 8d Hanger Nails	Connector	3	EA
5# 16d Galv. Nails	General Framing	3	EA
5# 8d Ctd. Box Nails	General Framing	1	EA

WALL FRAMING

Item	Location	Qty	UM
4x4 - 10' Treated	Post	4	EA
2x4 - 10' Std. & Btr. Doug. Fir	Shoe Nailer	6	EA
5# 16d Galv. Nails	General Framing	1	EA
5# 8d Ctd. Box Nails	General Framing	1	EA

ROOF FRAMING

Item	Location	Qty	UM
2x6 - 10' #2 & Btr. Doug. Fir	Beam	7	EA
2x6 - 8' #2 & Btr. Doug. Fir	Joist	26	EA
1/2" - CDX 5-Ply Plywood	Beam	1	EA
3/4" - Sq. Edge Plywood	Arch	6	EA
1/4" - 4x8 Plywood (Sanded)	Arch	1	EA
7/16" - 4x8 Plywood	Roof Decking	10	EA
15-lb. Roofing Felt	Roof	1	RL
Classic 3 - Tab 20-Year Shingle	Roof	10	BN
5# 16d Galv. Nails	General Framing	3	EA
5# 8d Zinc Coated Box Nails	General Framing	3	EA
5# 10d Bright Box Nails	General Framing	3	EA
5# 6d Galvanized Box Nails	General Framing	2	EA
5# 1/2" Roofing Nails	Roofing Felt	1	EA
5# 1-1/4" Roofing Nails	Shingle	2	EA
10 oz. - Paintable Caulk	Flashing	2	TB

FINISH/RAILING

Item	Location	Qty	UM
4x4 - 10' Treated	Post	1	EA
3/8"x4" Lag Screws	Post	4	EA
3/8"x1-1/2" Washer	Post	4	EA
2x6 - 12' Treated	Decking/Tread	29	EA
2x6 - 16' Treated	Decking/Tread	23	EA
2x4 - 8' Treated	Railing Cap	3	EA
2x4 - 10' Treated	Railing Cap	4	EA
1x3 - 8' Treated	Side Rail	12	EA
1x3 - 10' Treated	Side Rail	16	EA
2"x2" - 3' Sq. Cut Blstr.	Baluster	96	EA
2x3 - 8' Treated	Blstr. Blocking	6	EA
2x3 - 10' Treated	Blstr. Blocking	8	EA
2x12 - 6' Treated	Stringer	3	EA
3x5 Heavy Angle (A35)	Stringer	6	EA
5/16"x1-1/2" Lag Screws	Heavy Angle	24	EA
Stair Angle (TA10)	Tread	6	EA
Screen Mold (1/4"x3/4")	Screen	212	LF
Fiberglass Screen (48"x25')	Screen	7	RL
32"x80" Screen Door w/Hardware	Door	1	EA
Screen Door Hardware Kit	Door	1	EA
1/2"x1" Door Stop	Door	20	LF
1/4" - 4x8 Plywood (Sanded)	Soffit	1	EA
1x2 - 8' #2 & Btr. Doug. Fir	Top Post Trim	3	EA
1x6 - 8' #2 & Btr. Doug. Fir	Top Post Trim	2	EA
1x4 - 8' #2 & Btr. Doug. Fir	Post Wrap	20	EA
1x6 - 8' #2 & Btr. Doug. Fir	Post Wrap	20	EA
Decorative Wood Post Cap	Post	4	EA
1# 2-1/2" Ctd. Screws	Decking/Railing	10	EA
5# 16d Galv. Nails	General Framing	2	EA
5# 8d Ctd. Box Nails	General Framing	1	EA
5# 4d Galvanized Finish Nails	Finish Framing	1	EA
5# 6d Galvanized Finish Nails	Finish Framing	3	EA
5# 8d Galvanized Finish Nails	Finish Framing	3	EA
Construction Adhesive	General Framing	2	TB

Picture Credits

GLOSSARY

Analogous shades
Colors bordering each other on the color spectrum; e.g., yellow and orange, blue and purple.

Anchor bolt
A J-shaped bolt used mainly to fasten sill plates to the concrete piers or foundation slab of an outdoor structure. The curved end of the bolt is embedded in the concrete. The threaded section projecting upward attaches to the sill plate.

Annuals
Plants that complete their full life cycle in one growing season.

Baluster
Vertical member of railings, usually made from 2x2 lumber and fastened to rails spanning two or more posts.

Batterboard
A wooden assembly made up of two stakes and a third board spanning horizontally between them; used with mason's line to lay out structures.

Blocking
Lengths of 2x4 fastened between joists to add support and structural rigidity on long spans.

Complementary colors
Opposing colors, such as blue and orange or red and green, that when placed together create a sense of balance.

Decay resistant
Refers to wood that is either naturally resistant to rot—such as cedar and redwood—or treated with chemicals to be rot-resistant.

Detail
Part of a building plan showing a cutaway section of a particular view and revealing hidden elements.

Dimensional lumber
Graded for strength, this lumber is intended for the understructure of a playhouse, shed or gazebo or for fence posts and arbor corners; it ranges in nominal size from 2 to 4 inches in width and is at least 2 inches thick.

Downspout
A pipe, made of metal or vinyl, that channels water running off the roof from the gutters to the ground away from the foundation.

Easement
A section of property that must be left accessible for others to use.

Elevation
Part of a building plan that shows a side view. Included in the view are dimensions, materials and, in some cases, a detail of the view.

Exposure rating
The rating given exterior plywood panels based on their tolerance to moisture.

Face-nail
To drive a nail through the face of one board into another, with the nail perpendicular to the surface.

Footing
The wide concrete base under a concrete pier; serves to hold the pier firmly in place.

Framing connector
Metal hardware that is used to connect structural members to form a stronger joint than is possible with conventional fasteners.

Framing plan
The part of a building plan that shows the dimensions and types of materials used for the understructure.

Frost line
The depth below grade to which the ground freezes in winter.

Galvanized
A process by which fasteners are coated with zinc to prevent oxidization due to contact with moisture. Hot-dipped galvanized fasteners are the highest quality.

Grade
The slope or incline of the ground; usually expressed in vertical inches per horizontal foot.

Ground-fault circuit interrupter (GFCI)
An electrical device that shuts off power to a circuit when current leakage is detected. Usually required in outdoor wiring.

Gutter
A trough, made of metal or vinyl, fastened to the fascia below the eaves, designed to carry water running off the roof to a downspout.

Heartwood
The wood nearest the center of a tree. In redwood and cedar, it is the wood most resistant to decay and generally considered the highest in quality.

Height limit
A zoning bylaw that sets a limit on the height of a structure on your property.

Lien releases
A contractual stipulation releasing the property owner from costs incurred by the contractor.

Lot-coverage limit
A legal restriction governing what proportion of your property a structure can cover.

On center
The span from the center of one supporting member to the center of another. Abbreviated on building plans as "o.c."

Overhead
A structure built over a doorway or landing for shade or privacy.

Perennials
Plants that live through a minimum of three growing seasons.

Pier
A cylindrical concrete foundation member set below ground level to support a structure.

Plan view
A view of the structure seen from directly above, indicating mainly the dimensions of the structure's perimeter.

Pressure-treated
A process by which chemical preservatives are forced into lumber under pressure, making it resistant to decay and insect damage.

Rendering
An artist's representation of the finished project.

Setback
A legal restriction governing how close to your property line a structure can be built.

Site plan
A complete map of a lot indicating the position of all structures, including the proposed new one.

Skids
A portable foundation structure built for a small shed, playhouse or other four-sided structure.

Span
The distance from the center of one supporting member to the center of another.

Stucco
A siding material made of a mixture of portland cement, lime, sand and water.

Toenail
To fasten two wood pieces together with a nail driven in at an angle.

Understructure
The supporting structure of a playhouse, gazebo or other structure made up of the piers or foundation and joists.

Wood composite
An outdoor building material made from a 50/50 blend of wood and recycled plastic.